Contents

Introduction

Aims

This book has been compiled as a 'cookbook of ideas' for
- riding instructors, in particular trainee Assistant Instructors,
- riders schooling their own horses and ponies, and
- parents supervising young riders.

The selection of exercises given here shows how to make imaginative and constructive use of a 20m × 40m schooling area, adding variety and interest to lessons and riding sessions for all concerned — teachers, riders *and* horses.

Structure of this Book

This book is divided into a number of sections, containing a selection of exercises which logically form a category or group. Inevitably, some exercises could fall easily into one or two categories — for example, Exercise 5.1 could be described as two half circles or as a two-loop serpentine. In such cases, the classification is somewhat arbitrary. The way in which the exercises have been grouped can be seen from the contents page. However, other ways of grouping the exercises do exist (e.g. novice riders, transitions, half a school, open order, etc.), so a cross-reference section linking exercises in this way is provided at the back of the book.

Each section begins with an introduction which gives:
- an explanation of the purpose of the exercises in the section;
- a detailed description of a specimen exercise;
- a list of preparations;
- the aids;
- the words of command;
- the points of the exercise; and
- some hints on teaching the topic.

The remaining pages of each section detail the exercises, with relevant guide notes under five possible headings:
- Explanation.
- Safety.
- Likely problems.
- Variations.
- Comments.

General Note

The book assumes that you are working with horses that are quiet and well behaved. Also, do bear in mind that different horses are often trained to different aids for many of the lateral movements ('Should the inside leg be **on** or **behind** the girth for a turn on the forehand?'). This means that the aids that you give to your pupils need to be suitably modified.

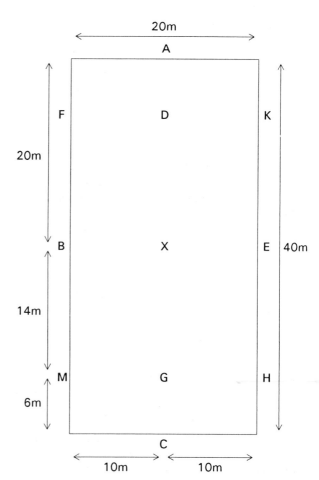

4

Teaching Notes

General Points

The lesson should be fun for all concerned: for you, for your riders, and for your horses.

The exercises should be appropriate to the level of fitness and training of both horse and rider.

Allow each exercise to go on just long enough for your riders to extract the maximum amount of benefit.

Use a range of different exercises.

Teaching many classes over a period of time will help you to become more confident in controlling the ride.

Watch the horses, the riders, and yourself.

Specific Points

Ensure that your commands are clear and unambiguous.

It is useful to practise the correct words of preparation and of command.

A correct form of words is given in the specimen exercise at the start of each section.

Allow sufficient time between the words of preparation and the words of command.

Check that the straight lines are ridden straight.

Check that all bends are ridden as part of a true circle, and that the sizes of circles and half-circles are correct.

Check that transitions occur in the correct place.

Check that figures are ridden in the correct place in the school: for example, a change of rein from A to C should be **on** the centre line.

Watch the rider's aids: head, shoulders, arms, elbows, wrists, hands, fingers, back, seat, legs, knees, ankles and feet.

Watch the rider's weight (is it central?).

Is the rider on the correct diagonal in rising trot?

Watch the horse: correct leading leg, bend, tempo, speed, impulsion and outline.

Assessing Riding Ability

Riders seeking instruction range from the complete beginner to the advanced competitor. Whilst you are unlikely to meet the latter early in your teaching career, you will almost certainly teach the former, as well as riders up to your own level of ability. It is useful to have a plan for assessing new riders (or even re-assessing familiar ones). Here is a suggested scheme.

A Basic Assessment

In the halt

Head on top of the shoulders? (i.e. not tipped forward or back)

Shoulders square? (i.e. not hunched, round-shouldered or twisted)

Back straight? (i.e. not bowed inwards or outwards, or bent left or right)

Back upright? (i.e. not tipping forward or back)

Elbow slightly in front of the body?

Straight line elbow-hand-bit?

Thumbs on top?

Pelvis central on saddle, both from beside and behind?

Knee below the knee roll (if flat-working)?

Lower leg on the girth?

Straight line head-hip-heel?

Heel horizontal with the toe?

Toe to the front?

In the walk

Do the rider's hands follow the horse's head movement?

Is the pelvis following the swing of the horse's back?

Are all the indicators that you looked for in the halt still just as good in the walk?

In the rising trot

Correct diagonal?

How high is the rise?

How soft is the return into the saddle?

In the sitting trot/canter

Has the lower leg started moving?

How 'still' is the upper body? (Look at the hands!)

While jumping

Does the rider fold and sit upright too soon or too late?

Do the hands 'give' to the horse's head?

Is the rider standing in the stirrups?

Is the rider folding from the waist?

Is the rider in front of or behind the movement?

Are the lower legs still and secure?

Is the rider looking up and ahead, or down at the fence?

Is he holding his breath?

Is the approach track correct?

Is the approach and get-away impulsive?

Through transitions
Does the rider tip forward or back?

Through turns
Is the inside leg on the girth?

Is the outside leg behind the girth?

Does the inside hand open?

Does the outside shoulder come round?

Rein-back
Does the horse remain straight?

Is the rhythm regular?

A Further Assessment
If, having done a basic assessment, your rider has no obvious areas for improvement, then you can try some of the following techniques to uncover any weaknesses.

Straight lines
Ask for a slower, more impulsive, tempo.

Ask for greater collection in each gait.

Ask for greater extension in each gait.

Circles
Use voltes, and watch the rider's head, shoulders, arms and legs.

Transitions
Direct upward transitions.

Direct downward transitions. Go as far as canter-to-halt if necessary.

Jumps
Raise the height of a fence.

Plan a more difficult turn from one fence to the next.

Shorten or lengthen the distance, requiring the rider to use greater collection or lengthening.

Ask the rider to canter on a named leg on landing.

Increasing the Variety of Exercises
Many of the exercises in this book have a lot of possible variations of both track and gait. An example of variation of track is a 20 metre circle at C being followed by a 20 metre circle at E. A change of gait would involve, for example, one circle being walked, with the other trotted. There are a lot of other variations which could be applied to most, if not all, of the exercises. A selection is listed below.

Variations of the rein
Riding with the reins in one hand (usually the outside hand).

Riding with the reins knotted, and both hands free of the reins.

Arm swinging.

Shoulder hunching.

Completely relaxed arm (should 'flop around' a little in the sitting trot).

Hand on head.

Rub-the-tummy-and-pat-the-head (needs both hands!)

Arms held horizontally, either in front or to the sides.

Variations of the stirrup
The following are always done with both feet out of the stirrups:

Ankle rotation.

Drawing circles in the air with the toe (usually with the toe going towards the horse's sides at the top of the circle).

'Walking' from the knee.

'Walking' from the hips.

Knees out, back and down.

Knees together (above the pommel), and 'throwing' them down.

Choice of Exercise
Most of the exercises featured in this book assume that you have full use of a 20m by 40m arena. However, you may need to share the school with another class, or avoid boggy patches in an outdoor manège. A list of exercises suitable for half an arena is given in the cross-reference listing at the end of the book. This listing also groups the exercises in other ways, such as transitions, and exercises suitable for the more advanced class.

A WORD OF WARNING
Not all the above variations are suitable for all exercises. For example, the knees-together-and-throw variation would be unsafe during a counter-canter (if it was even possible). Also, lead files may need to keep the reins in one hand while the rest of the class has knotted their reins. Use only those variations which your class can perform safely.

1. *Moving the Ride Around the School*

Aims
It is a means of moving from one place to another between performing various exercises.
It is a means of changing the rein.
It provides interest for both horses and riders.
It improves the fitness of both horse and riders.
It keeps the ride warm on a cold day.

General Points
Selecting a good lead file makes everybody's job easier.
Correct school figures should be used at all times.
Frequent changes of rein makes the work more interesting.
There are over eighty rein changes, some of which are illustrated overleaf.
Not all rein changes are suitable for novice horses or riders.
Give rest periods at walk or halt, depending upon the ability of the riders.

Choice of Exercises
Choose exercises with regard to such factors as:
Fitness, age and ability of horses and riders.
Riders' objectives.
How interesting is the work?
State of going — slippery? heavy? dusty?
Temperature of the day.
Level of light.

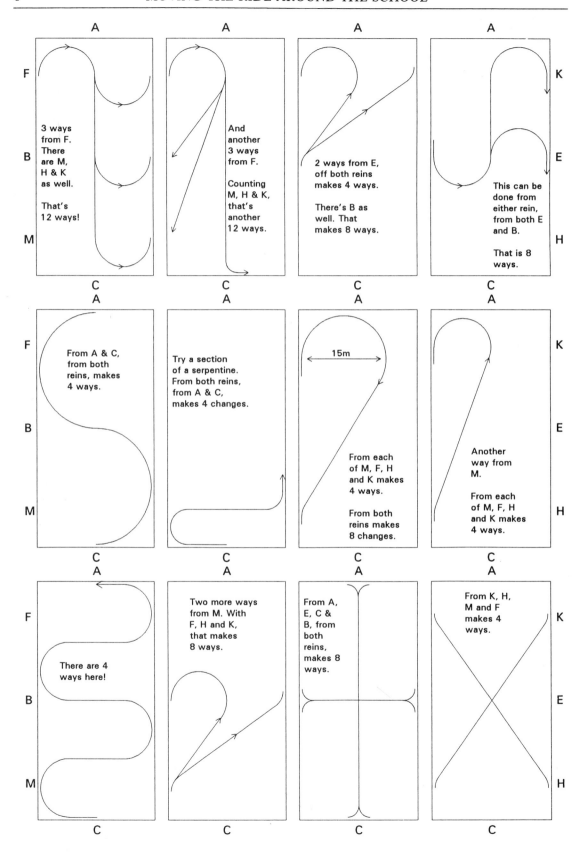

A SPECIMEN EXERCISE

The ride is going large, on the right rein, in walk.
Lead files successively go forward to working trot (sitting) at E, go forward to canter in the
   corner at H, and canter to the rear of the ride.

Preparations

Plan your track first.
Remind the riders of the aids if necessary.
Put your ride going large in walk.
Stand away from the track.
Give the words of command.

The Aids

For the trot:

Apply both legs equally on the girth.
Keep the rein contact even.

For the canter:

Inside leg on the girth.
Outside leg applied behind the girth.
Inside rein asks for the bend (in corners).
Outside rein controls the forward movement.

The Command

'Lead file go forward to working trot sitting at E. In corner after H go forward to canter.
Canter towards the rear of the ride, go forward to trot, and walk on reaching the rear.'

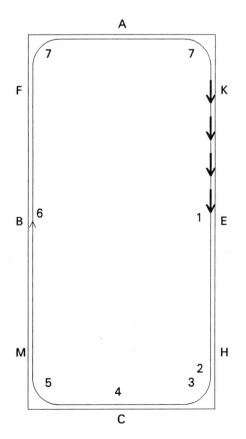

KEY

1. Sitting trot.
2. Position right.
3. Canter transition.
4. Go straight along the short side.
5. Go into the corner at M.
6. Canter straight along the long side.
7. Correct use of corners.

EXERCISE 1.1

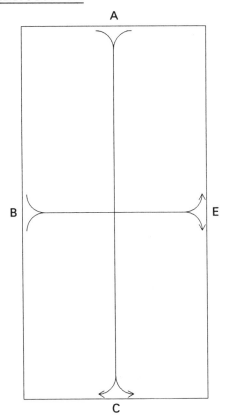

EXERCISE 1.2

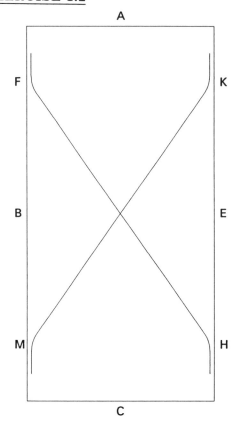

Explanation

Two methods of changing the rein by simple straight lines.

1. Up the centre line from A to C, or down the centre line from C to A.
2. Across the school from B to E, or from E to B.

These can be executed from either rein.

Explanation

Changing the rein along the long diagonals.
From the right rein: M - X - K and K - X - M.
From the left rein: F - X - H and H - X - F.

Likely problems

Turns too late.

Not going into the corners.

Rider attempts 'sharp turns', e.g. MXK or KXM from the left rein, or FXH or HXF from the right rein.

EXERCISE 1.3

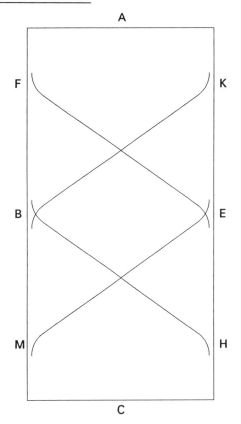

EXERCISE 1.4

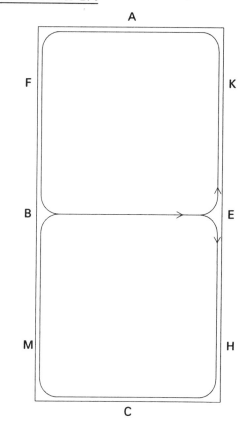

Explanation

Changing the rein by using the short diagonals:

Off the right rein	Off the left rein
M - E	F - E
B - K	B - H
K - B	H - B
E - M	E - F

Explanation

Riding squares — suitable for walk or trot.

Have the ride spaced out to one horse's length between them, and change (as a ride) from one square to the other every time the ride passes through X.

Likely problems

Horse not straight.
Badly ridden corners.

Variation

Number off the ride. Start the exercise as a single ride to establish the shape. On command odd numbers go onto one square, even numbers go onto the other square. Each rider then changes square every time he goes through X. (This is similar to Exercise 3.5, except that it is ridden on a square instead of a circle).

2. *Straight Lines*

Aims

Improves the horse (discourages napping, etc.).
Improves the rider's lateral balance.

General

The straight line is the simplest of all possible figures.
It is the first figure taught to all novice riders.
It must be used in conjunction with simple turns at the ends and sides of the school.
The straight line can be ridden at all gaits, as well as in the rein-back.

Riding a Straight Line

Riding a truly straight line is a difficult exercise.
It shows up lateral imbalance in both horse and rider.
When ridden along any side, a lot of horses proceed with their shoulders 'on the boards',
  especially in canter.

How to Teach

Start with straight lines along the long side of the school.
Encourage riders to 'fix their eye' on the point where they are going. If they can see outside the
  school, ask them to line up a point on the edge of the school with an object (e.g. a tree)
  outside the school.
The exercise becomes more demanding if ridden:
  on the centre line;
  on the threequarter line;
  2m off a long side;
  0.5m off a long side.

A SPECIMEN EXERCISE

The ride is going large, on the right rein, in walk.

Lead files successively track right at A, trot at X, track right at C, and trot large to the rear of the ride.

Preparations

Plan your track first.
Remind the riders of the aids if necessary.
Put your ride going large in walk.
Stand away from the track and the centre line.
Give the words of command.

The Aids

For the turns

Inside leg on the girth.
Inside hip forward.
Outside leg behind the girth.
Outside shoulder forward.
Inside rein controls the bend.
Outside rein controls the forward movement.

For the straight line

Both legs on the girth.
Both reins held equally.
Rider's weight central in the saddle.

The Command

'Lead files in succession track right up the centre line at A. At X trot. At C track right, trot large, and go forwards to walk on reaching the rear of the ride.'

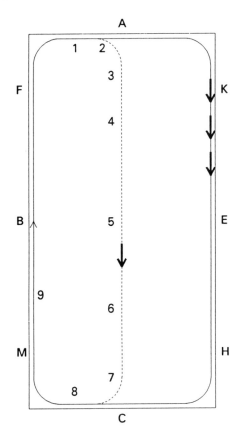

KEY

1. Prepare for the turn.
2. Turning before A, to go directly onto the centre line.
3. Neither overshoot nor undershoot the centre line.
4. Proceed straight; all aids applied equally to both sides of the horse.
5. Trot at X, neither early nor late.
6. Keep the straight track.
7. Go right up to C before asking for the turn.
8. Go straight before the corner at M.
9. Go straight along the MBF long side.

EXERCISE 2.1

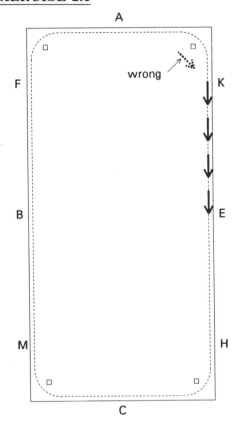

EXERCISE 2.2

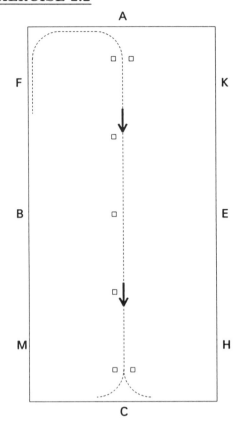

Explanation

Put a block or cone in each corner. Have the ride walking or trotting large around the school in either open or closed order.

Safety!

Old tin cans and similar items must **not** be used. Plastic or rubber objects are best, failing which trotting poles can be used.

Likely problem

Horse goes on the inside of a block (see diagram).

Comment

Very useful for children — it encourages them to go into the corners.

Explanation

This exercise is suitable for rides of up to four riders. Assemble some blocks or cones 0.5m clear of the line A - C (see diagram). With the ride in open order, track up the centre line, sometimes changing the rein at C depending on the instructor's call. Continue the exercise with fewer blocks.

Likely problem

Straight lines deteriorate as blocks are removed.

Comment

This is a useful exercise for re-affirming how a straight line should be ridden.

EXERCISE 2.3

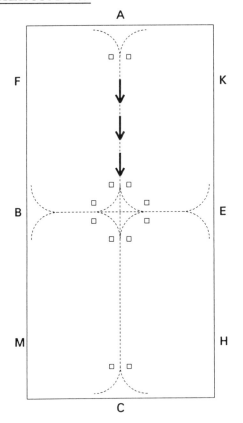

EXERCISE 2.4

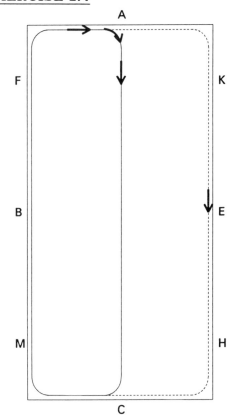

Explanation

This exercise is suitable for young riders in a game of 'follow my leader'. Assemble some blocks or cones as shown in the diagram. With the ride walking or trotting in closed order, lead file selects a path between the blocks.

Likely problems

Lead file forgets to use different figures.
Riders go on the wrong side of some blocks.
Ride spreads out into open order.

Explanation

Ride in either open or closed order on a rectangle in one side of the school in trot. Individuals on command go large at A, canter K to H, trot, and rejoin the ride.

Likely problems

Lines not straight.
New lead file may try to follow the person doing the exercise if the ride is working in closed order.

Safety!

The person doing the exercise **must** be capable of going from canter to trot at or before H.
Walk or halt the ride if necessary to allow the rider to rejoin the ride.

Variation

For a novice ride, the main ride could be in walk, and the person doing the exercise could be in trot.

EXERCISE 2.5

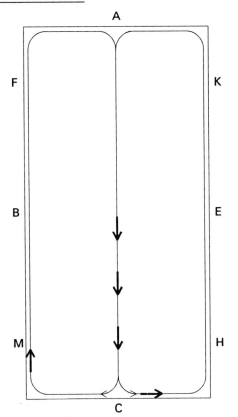

EXERCISE 2.6

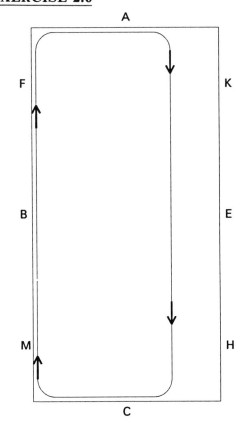

Explanation
Number off the ride.

Lead file takes the ride up the centre line.

At C, even numbers go right, odd numbers go left.

Continue tracking up the centre line. Every time the split rides meet at A, riders slot into their original order, changing the rein every time at C.

The ride must watch their dressings and adjust the speed as necessary to avoid problems at A.

Likely problems
Getting in a muddle at A.

Not going right up to C.

Dressings not maintained.

Explanation
Ride goes up the threequarter line in open order. This helps to teach the horses not to go 'on the boards'.

Likely problems
Riders turning too early/late.

Poor turns.

Lines not straight.

Horses not straight.

Comments
You can get a better view of what is happening by placing yourself at one end of the three-quarter line.

Useful for teaching the rider to 'go straight'.

EXERCISE 2.7

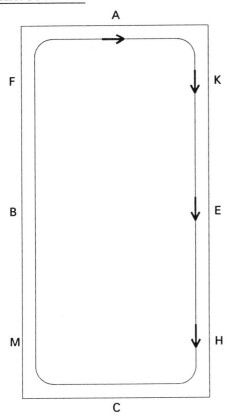

EXERCISE 2.8

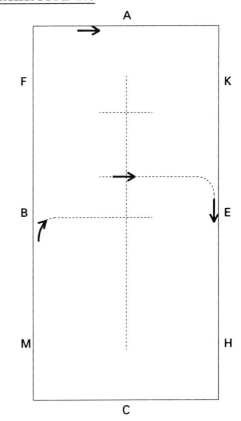

Explanation
Ride go large on the inner track, with one marker's distance between each of the horses. Use transitions halt-walk and walk-trot. As with the previous exercise, the idea is to prevent the horses going 'on the boards'.

Likely problems
Distances between horses changing.
Horses drifting back to the boards.

Variation
Can be ridden with the reins in one hand.

Explanation
Ride in open order at walk. Turn across at will from any point on either long side and include a transition to halt on the centre line. Rider continues on the same rein after resuming walk.

Likely problems
Accuracy of transition.
Riders moving off (from the centre line) when there is insufficient space for them to rejoin the ride.
Individual rider always turning at the same point.

Variation
Ride in trot, include downward transition to walk 2m before centre line, upward transition 2m after the centre line, possibly include a halt.

EXERCISE 2.9

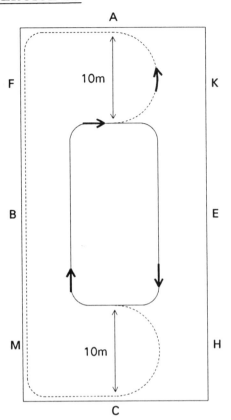

EXERCISE 2.10

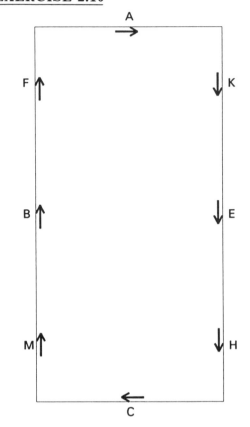

Explanation
Ride in walk on a rectangle in the middle of the school. Individuals on command go forward to trot and ride half a 10m circle to A, trot to C, half a 10m circle to rejoin ride in walk. The riders on the rectangle must give way to the person rejoining the ride.

Likely problem
Half circle leaving the rectangle is a poor shape.

Variation
For advanced riders, you can have the half circle in trot, canter at A, go large, trot and turn at A or C, and rejoin the ride.

Explanation
This exercise is for a maximum of eight riders. Halt the ride from the rear, at one marker's distance apart. Move the whole ride forward simultaneously into walk, and then into trot. Get the ride to work on maintaining distances, and include transitions through halt, walk and trot.

Likely problems
Riders getting too close to one another.
Poor transitions.

Variations
With advanced riders you can include 10m circles between the transitions — with the trot circles ridden sitting.

EXERCISE 2.11

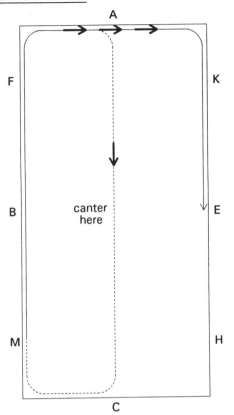

EXERCISE 2.12

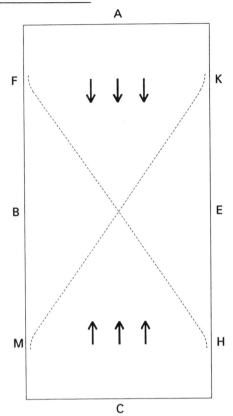

Explanation
In closed order ride go large in walk. Lead files in succession turn onto the centre line at A, go forward to working trot (sitting), canter at X, go straight to C, there turning to take rear file.

Likely problems
Wrong canter lead.
Late strike-off.
Crooked line.

Variation
Halt the ride on a threequarter line, and use the same figure to develop a simple change of leg exercise, trotting through X.

Comments
As part of the warm-up for this exercise: ride goes large, lead files canter at E or B, and take rear file.
Useful as an exercise to reduce reliance on corners to produce the correct bend, and for obtaining the correct canter lead.

Explanation
Using the diagonals as an alternative to circles for riding a simple change through trot. See Exercises 2.11 and 3.4.

Likely problems
Wrong canter lead.
Poor corners, particularly after the simple change.

Comment
Suitable only for fairly advanced riders.

EXERCISE 2.13

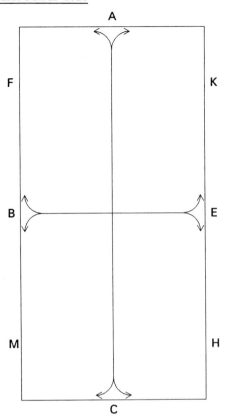

EXERCISE 2.14

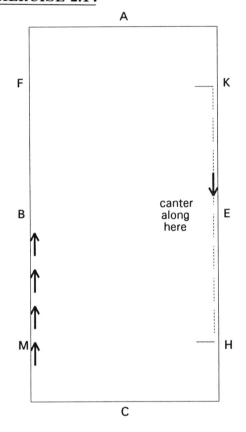

Explanation

This is a good exercise for warming up. Have the ride going large in trot. Lead files in succession change the rein by any correct school figure they choose, and then canter or turn across the school to take the rear.

Likely problem

Lead files can't think of any rein changes. (See page 8.)

Comments

Useful for novice riders. They often forget to change the diagonal. This exercise can be used to establish changing the diagonal firmly in their minds during the warm-up period.

Explanation

Lead files in succession canter and count the number of strides between K - H. Change the rein. Repeat the exercise, asking for a little lengthening, again counting strides. See if there is a difference.

Likely problem

After H (or K) the horse may rush towards the back of the ride, particularly after the lengthening.

Variation

Ask for shortened strides.

EXERCISE 2.15

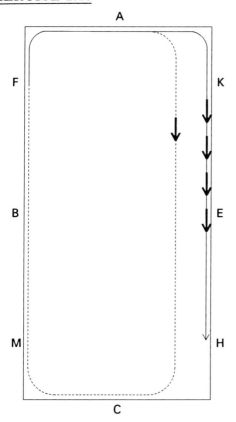

EXERCISE 2.16

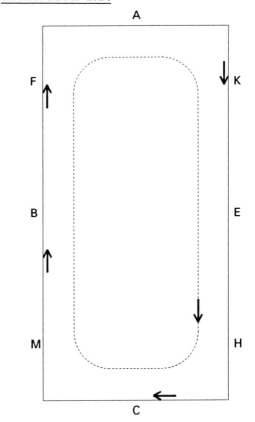

Explanation
With the ride in trot, **rear** files come onto the inner track, canter past the ride, go large around the school, pass the ride (again), and take lead file (in trot).

Safety!
The person doing the exercise must come **well** onto the inner track when going past the ride.

Variations
Ride in walk.
Canter from the rear of the ride to the front of the ride. (Less effort required from the rider; takes less time to execute.)

Explanation
Ride spaced out in open order in walk. On command, individuals come well onto the inner track, go forward to canter, canter once round the school on the inner track, and retake their place in the ride.

Safety!
This exercise must not be used if any horse is a known kicker.

Likely problem
Rider not coming far enough onto the inner track.

Variation
For novice riders, perform the inner track exercise in trot with the rest of the ride in the walk.

EXERCISE 2.17

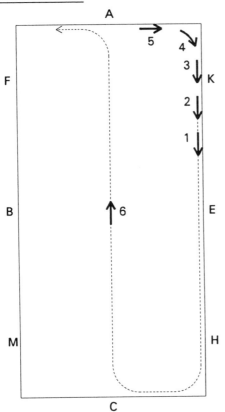

EXERCISE 2.18

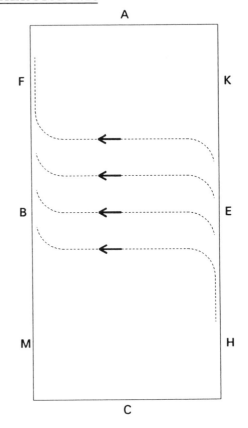

Explanation

Ride turns down centre line in trot every time they reach C. Rear file halts at X and waits for the ride. As they approach, go forward to walk and trot as the new lead file, and change the rein. The new rear file halts at X. The exercise continues until the original lead file is back in front.

Likely problems

Halts not at X.
Halts not square.
Halts fidgety.
Rider moves off too soon (usually) or too late (sometimes).
New lead file forgets to change the rein.

Explanation

Have the ride walking large in closed order. On command, the whole ride simultaneously turns across the school to change the rein.

Likely problems

Ride does not turn simultaneously.
Dressings deteriorate.
Riders drift towards one another.

Variations

Can be ridden from trot (when riders are reasonably practised at the walk).
Turn back to the same rein (reverses the order of the ride).

3. 20 Metre Circles

Aims
Lateral flexion for the horse.
Encourages softening of the horse's side to the rider's leg.
Enables pupils to work on producing a consistent bend.

General Points
The 20m circle is **circular**.
The 20m circle about X touches the outer track at B and E for exactly one stride. It also passes exactly half-way between X and A, and between X and C.
The 20m circle at A touches the track at A and again halfway between E and the corner, passes directly over the X marker, and touches the track again halfway between B and the corner. It does not touch the track at either F or K.
20m circles always start at A, E, C or B. (Two 20m circles are illustrated below.)

Riding a 20m Circle
Riding a truly circular circle is a difficult exercise.
Circles show up any stiffness in both horse and rider.
When ridden on both reins, circles reveal any unevenness of bend in both horse and rider.
The horse should be bent throughout his entire body, following the curve of the circle.
The horse's hind feet go in the same track as his front feet.
The rider's shoulders match the horse's shoulders.

How to Teach
Halt the ride.
Walk the circle yourself.
Explain the aids.
Mention the four circle points.
Mention that the bend remains constant.

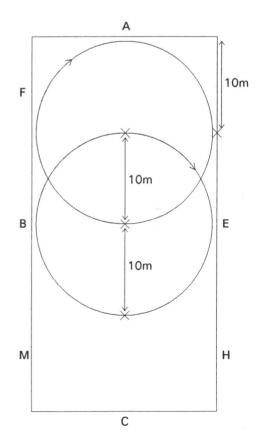

A SPECIMEN EXERCISE
The ride is going large, on the left rein.
The ride commences a 20m circle at E, executes one circle, and then goes large.

Preparations
Plan your track first.
Remind the riders of the aids if necessary.
Have your ride going large in an appropriate gait.
Stand away from the track.
Give the words of command.

The Aids
Left rein asks for the bend.
Right rein goes forward, allowing the horse to bend, but still supporting the horse.
Left leg is applied on the girth, asking for impulsion and a bend through the horse's body.
Right leg is applied behind the girth to prevent the hindquarters swinging out.
Left hip is forward to move the rider's weight **slightly** to the inside of the circle.

The Command
'At E, the whole ride commence a 20m circle. Ride one circle, and then go large.'

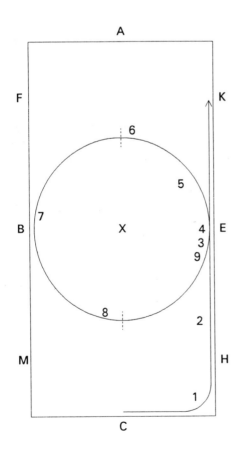

KEY
1. Ride a good corner.
2. Think of the shape of the circle. Ask for position left.
3. Before E, half-halt, and look at the next tangent point.
4. Commence the circle.
5. Maintain a good rhythm. Look around your circle.
6. Before the centre line, half-halt and look towards B. Cross the centre line halfway between X and A.
7. Before B, half-halt and look at the next tangent point.
8. Before the centre line, half-halt and look towards E. Cross the centre line halfway between X and C.
9. Half-halt, go straight and large.

EXERCISE 3.1

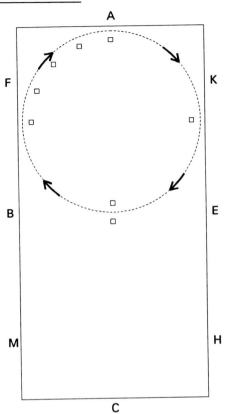

EXERCISE 3.2

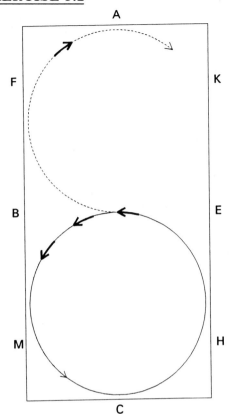

Explanation

Assemble some blocks 0.5m inside a 20m circle at A. With the ride in open order in either walk or trot, commence riding the 20m circle. After four or five circles, go large. Remove every other block, and repeat the exercise.

Likely problems

Riders go too far into the corners.
Loss of circle shape as blocks are removed.

Variation

For private or semi-private lessons, the 20m circle can be cantered — but **do** bring the blocks another 0.5m in from the track (to avoid the risk of the horse kicking them).

Comment

This exercise is useful for re-affirming how a true circle should be ridden.

Explanation

Put the ride onto a 20m circle at C on the left rein in walk. Lead file tracks right at X, trots the circle at A, and rejoins the rear of the ride.

Likely problems

New lead-file horse attempts to follow the person doing the exercise.
Poor path through X.

Variation

Ride at C in trot. Lead files in succession canter a circle to A (from X), and rejoin the ride through X.

EXERCISE 3.3

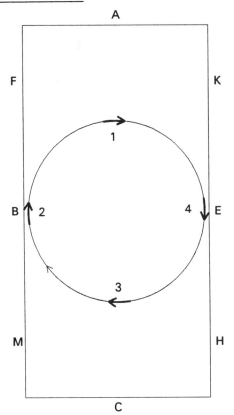

EXERCISE 3.4

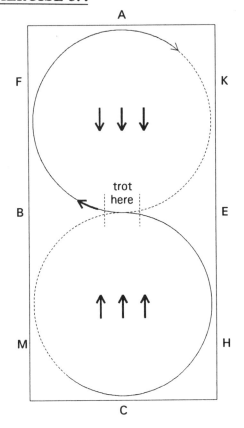

Explanation
Have the ride in walk on a 20m circle. Starting from the rear of the ride, ask riders to halt at a given circle point. With the ride continuing on the circle, command transitions either directly or progressively between halt-walk-trot.

Likely problem
Distances may drift apart; correct by lengthening or shortening stride where necessary.

Variations
Use any of the large circle points.
Can be ridden on both reins.

Comments
Suitable only for rides of four or eight. If eight riders, use circles at A and C only.
You can see both sides of the riders if you stand outside the circle/s.

Explanation
This exercise is called 'simple change [of leg through trot]'. Halt the ride on two lines as shown in the diagram. Call each rider in turn to:
- go onto a 20m circle at A;
- establish a canter;
- 3m before X, establish trot;
- go onto the circle at C;
- establish canter as soon as possible after X;
- change the rein and canter lead every time the rider passes through X.

Likely problems
Poor canter strike-off.
Wrong canter lead.
Path not passing through X.
Path not straight through X
Poor circles.

Variation
For horses who anticipate a lot, ask the rider sometimes to stay on the same circle.

EXERCISE 3.5

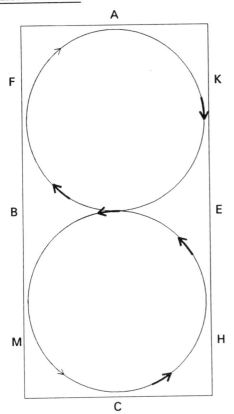

EXERCISE 3.6

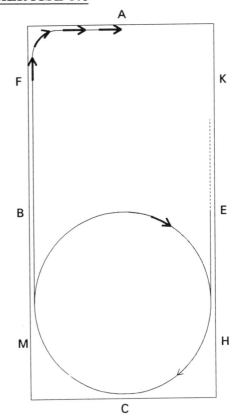

Explanation

Number off the ride. Ride a figure of eight with odd numbers going left at X and even numbers going right at X. Riders change the rein every time they go through X. The ride should go through X in the same order every time.

Likely problems

Speeds may vary, causing distances between riders to change. Each rider must ride with consideration for the person before them and the person behind them through X.

Comment

With novices start in walk before trying this exercise in trot.

Explanation

Have the ride in walk in closed order. Lead file goes forward to trot and canter, then includes a 20m circle (in canter) from any point before joining the rear of the ride.

Likely problems

The new lead-file horse may try to follow the horse doing the exercise.

Poor circle shape — but the person doing the exercise must come on the inner track if the path of the ride threatens to interfere with the circle. New lead file should halt the ride if this is likely to happen.

EXERCISE 3.7

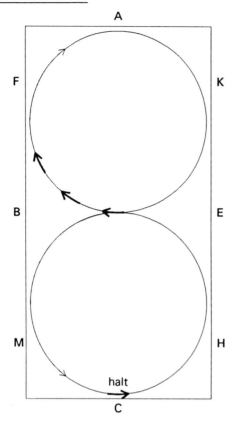

EXERCISE 3.8

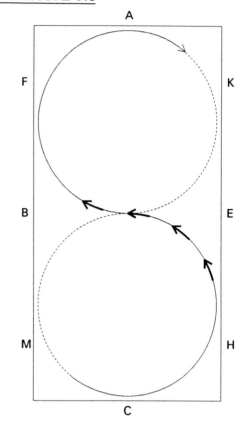

Explanation
Ride in walk, closed order, on a 20m circle at A on the right rein. Lead files in succession trot at X and circle on the left rein to C, the rest of the ride staying on the circle at A. Upon reaching C rider halts for 4 seconds, goes forward to trot and rejoins the ride passing through X.

Likely problems
Halt fidgety.
Second horse may try to follow the lead file after
    X.

Explanation
The whole ride rides a simple figure of eight using the two 20m circles at A and C, changing from one circle to the other each time they pass through X. Can be ridden in walk or trot.

Likely problems
Weight aids applied incorrectly.
Not straight through X.
Path not going over X.

Variation
Can be ridden in semi-open order.

Comment
Helps to establish in the riders' minds the location of the centre of the school.

EXERCISE 3.9

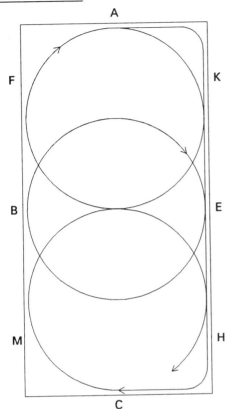

EXERCISE 3.10

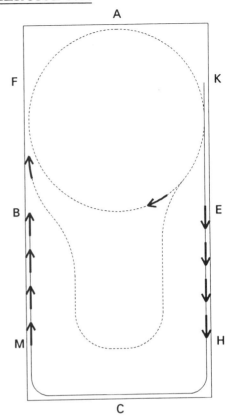

Explanation
Ride in closed order, ride one 20m circle at A, go large and ride one 20m circle at E/B, go large and ride one 20m circle at C.

Likely problems
Poor circle shapes.
Ride getting too spaced out.

Variations
Suitable only for ride in closed order and in walk or trot.
Can be adapted to include some canter for private lessons.

Explanation
With the ride in trot, **rear** files commence a 20m circle in canter after K, ride one circle, go past the ride, and take lead file.

Safety!
The person doing the exercise must come well onto the inner track.

Likely problems
Horse won't go onto the circle.
Wrong canter lead.
Canter breaks as the rider approaches the ride.

EXERCISE 3.11

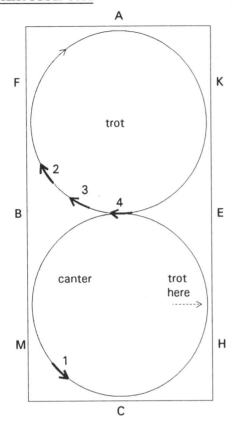

EXERCISE 3.12

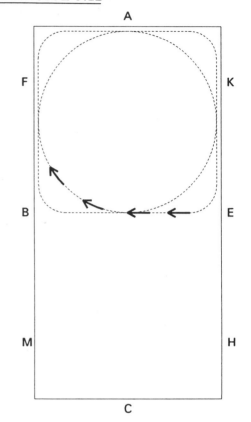

Explanation

Ride commence a 20m circle on the right rein from A in trot. Ride remains on trot circle and lead files in succession track left at X, canter and ride a 20m circle to C, trot after passing the H marker, join rear of the ride on the circle at A.

Likely problems

Poor circle shapes.
Late canter strike-off.
Wrong canter lead.
Rejoining ride badly.
Ride on trot circle loses form.

Variations

Change end of school.
Change the rein.

Comment

Not to be used for too novice a standard.

Explanation

With the ride in open or closed order on the right rein, walk or trot successive 20m circles and 20m squares, changing between each figure at X.

Likely problems

Circle poor shape.
Sides of the square not straight.
Failure to change to and from position right at X.

Comments

The object of this exercise is to demonstrate the difference between circles and squares.
Useful if you have only half a school in which to work.

4. Smaller Circles

Aims
Improves the horse's balance.
Improves the rider's balance.
Continues the suppling of the horse's side begun on the 20m circle exercises.
Serves as a preparation for leg yielding between the 10m and 20m circle.

General Points
A 15m circle ridden from either A or C comes 2.5m in from the long sides of the school.
A 15m circle ridden from either long side passes over the threequarter line for exactly one stride.
Any 10m circle ridden from either long side passes over the centre line for exactly one stride.
A 10m circle ridden from M, F, K or H clears the end of the school by exactly 1m.

Riding a Smaller Circle
The comments that apply to riding a 20m circle also apply to smaller circles.
All trot circles of 10m or less must be ridden in sitting trot.
Horse's inside shoulder often falls into the middle of the circle.

How to Teach
Halt the ride.
Walk the circle yourself.
Explain the aids.

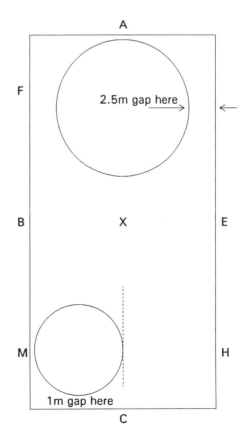

A SPECIMEN EXERCISE
The ride is going large, on the right rein, in trot.
The ride commences a 20m circle at B and executes one circle.
On returning to B, ride executes a 10m circle and then goes large.

Preparations
Plan your track first.
Remind the riders of the aids if necessary.
Have your ride going large in an appropriate gait.
Stand away from the track and the circles.
Give the words of command.

The Aids
Right rein asks for the bend.
Left rein goes forward, allowing the horse to bend, but still supporting the horse.
Right leg is applied on the girth, asking for impulsion and a bend through the horse's body.
Left leg is applied behind the girth to prevent the hindquarters swinging out.
Right hip is forward to move the rider's weight slightly to the inside of the circle.

The Command
'At B, the whole ride commence a 20m circle. Ride one circle. On returning to B, commence a 10m circle, working trot sitting, and then go large.'

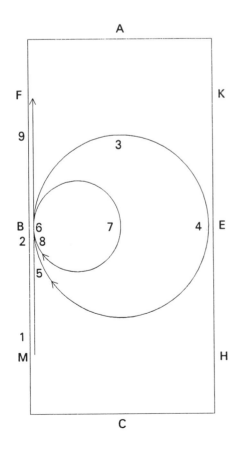

KEY
1. Good, active trot.
2. Think of the shape of the circle. Ask for position right.
3. Maintain a good shape to the circle.
4. One stride on the track at E.
5. Half-halt before B.
6. One stride on the track at B, and asking for more bend to the inside.
7. Passing through X, looking straight at C for one stride.
8. Half-halt before B.
9. Go straight and large.

EXERCISE 4.1

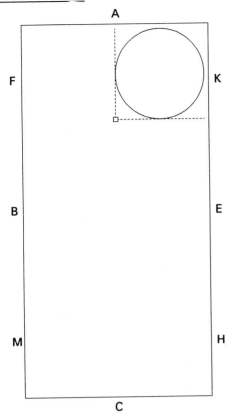

EXERCISE 4.2

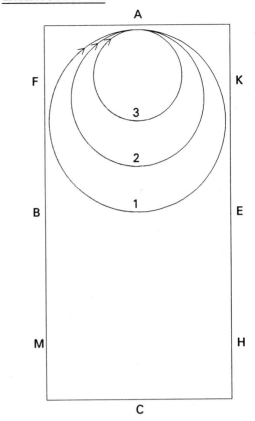

Explanation

Put a block or cone 10m from A on the centre line. With the ride walking or trotting in closed order, ride a 10m circle in the K corner. If trotted, it must be sitting.

Likely problems

Loss of impulsion.
Poor circle shape.
Rider goes outside the block.

Comment

The block helps the riders to see where the circle touches the edges of the 10m square.

Explanation

Same as the specimen exercise (page 32) but including a 15m circle.

Likely problem

Poor circle shapes.

Variations

Can be ridden as:
    20m - 15m - 10m - 15m - 20m - 15m - 10m etc.
or:
    20m - 15m - 10m - 20m - 15m - 10m - 20m etc.,
depending on instructor's call.

EXERCISE 4.3

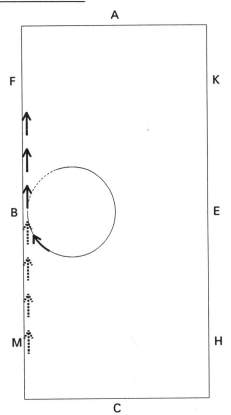

EXERCISE 4.4

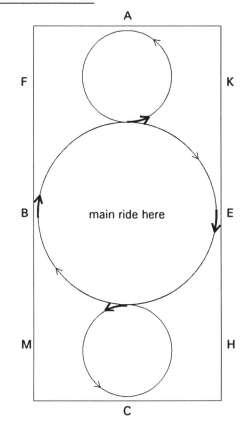

Explanation

Have the ride walking or trotting large. On command, lead file rides a 10m circle, taking rear file. If ridden in trot, it must be sitting. If there are more than four riders, the circle must be made larger.

Likely problems

Poor circle shape.
Circle too large or too small.

Explanation

Put the ride on a 20m circle at B/E in closed or open order in walk or trot. On command, each rider rides a 10m circle to A or C.

Likely problems

Poor circle shapes, particularly on the small circles.
Incorrect bend in the horses.
Rider's weight slipping on the small circle.

Comment

Riders on the large circle should allow for individuals to rejoin the ride.

EXERCISE 4.5

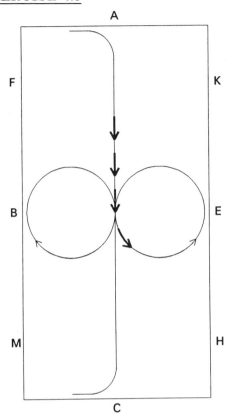

EXERCISE 4.6

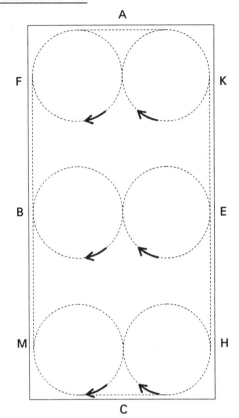

Explanation

The ride goes up the centre line from A, at X executes a single 10m circle to the left (i.e. towards E), then immediately executes a single 10m circle to the right (also from X). Can be ridden in walk or trot. If trotted, the circles must be ridden sitting.

Likely problems

Late turn off the centre line.
Loss of impulsion.
Poor circle shapes.

Variations

Start from C.
Change the rein.
Initiate the two circles at D, G or anywhere in between.

Explanation

Have the ride walking in open order. On reaching a corner or the middle of a long side, each rider rides a 10m circle. If two riders come too close to one another near the centre line, each must ride a slightly smaller (9m) circle.

Likely problems

Poor circle shapes.
Late turns onto the circles.

Variation

Can be done in trot, in which case the circles must be ridden sitting.

EXERCISE 4.7

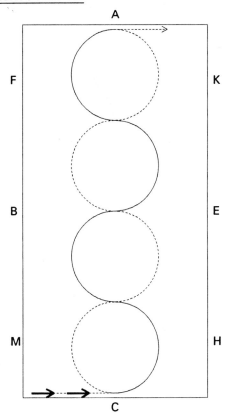

Explanation
Suitable for small rides, maximum of four riders. Walking in closed order, start riding 10m half circles from C. At the completion of each half circle, go onto the next. At A go large or return to C riding 10m half circles.

Likely problems
Ride gets lost. (Use a good lead file.)
Poor circle shapes.

Variation
Can be ridden in sitting trot.

Comment
Exercises 6.4 and 6.7 serve as useful warm-ups for this exercise.

EXERCISE 4.8

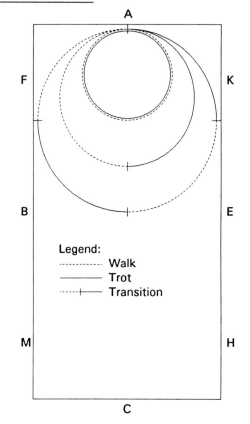

Legend:
-------- Walk
———— Trot
---+--- Transition

Explanation
This exercise is best suited to either one or two riders working in open order. Ride successive 20m, 15m and 10m circles, with transitions between walk and trot along the way. If there are two riders, have one circling at C while the other circles at A.

Likely problems
Poor circle shapes.
Late transitions.

Comment
This is a very useful exercise for getting horses to listen to the rider's leg.

EXERCISE 4.9

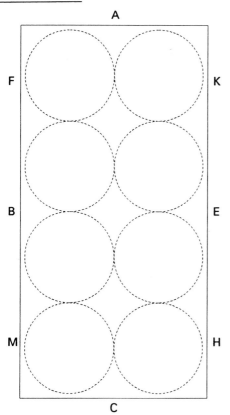

EXERCISE 4.10

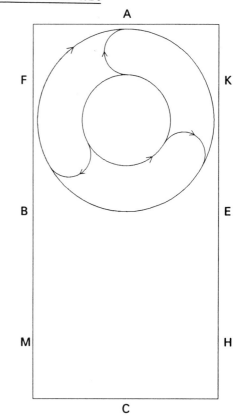

Explanation
Divide the school into eight circles, each of 10m diameter. Have the ride in walk or sitting trot in closed order. Lead file moves from one circle to another, with the rest of the ride following. No more than one and threequarter circles allowed on any circle.

Likely problems
Poor circle shapes.
Ride breaks up into open order.

Comments
Can only be used for more advanced riders.
Useful for horses who anticipate.
Improves lateral suppleness.

Explanation
Changing the rein by riding small outward half circles — must be performed in walk only.

Likely problems
Poor circle shape (on the 10m circle).
Small outward half circle late, or poor shape.

5. *Half Circles and Inclines*

Aims
Introduces movements which are not supported by the boards.

General Points

Half circle
The half circle is circular throughout its length.
The half circle goes through exactly 180 degrees.
When going from one half circle to another, there should be one straight stride parallel to a side of the school (see diagram).

Incline
The incline is straight throughout its length.
The incline stops short of the long side.
The transition from riding an incline to going large on the track is by means of an arc.
The arc is evenly curved throughout its length.

Half circle and diagonal incline
The half circle is 'extended' slightly, depending upon its size.
The incline starts after the centre line for 10m half circles, and after the threequarter line for 15m half circles.

Riding Half Circles and Inclines
The rhythm and impulsion should be the same throughout the exercise.
The horse's body should follow the curve of the half circle, and should be straight through the incline.
The horse should bend through the arc at the end of the incline.

How to Teach
Halt the ride.
Walk the half circle and diagonal incline yourself.
Explain the aids.
Use a cone to mark the size of the half circle if your riders need a visual aid.

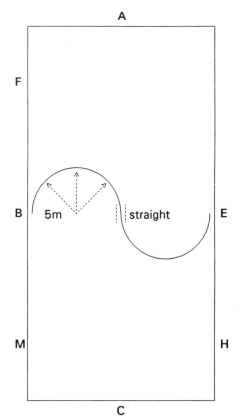

A SPECIMEN EXERCISE
The ride goes large, on the right rein, in trot.
At F, lead file executes a half 10m circle, and inclines back to M, changing the rein.

Preparations
Plan your track first.
Remind the riders of the aids if necessary.
Put your ride going large in an appropriate gait.
Stand away from the track and the line of the exercise.
Give the words of command.

The Aids
Right rein asks for the bend.
Left rein goes forward, allowing the horse to bend, but still supporting the horse.
Right leg is applied on the girth, asking for impulsion and a bend through the horse's body.
Left leg is applied behind the girth to prevent the hindquarters swinging out.
Right hip is forward to move the rider's weight slightly to the inside of the circle.

The Command
'At F, the whole ride commence a 10m half circle, and then incline back to the track at M.'

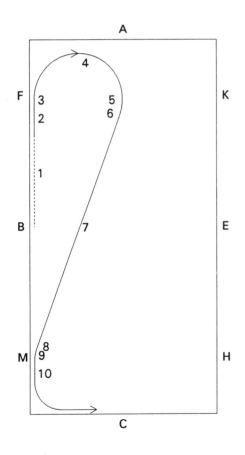

KEY
1. Good, active trot (sitting).
2. Position right.
3. Half-halt.
4. Maintain a good shape to the circle.
5. One stride on the centre line at D.
6. Half-halt.
7. Straight line towards M.
8. Half-halt.
9. Good turn.
10. Go straight, and large.

EXERCISE 5.1

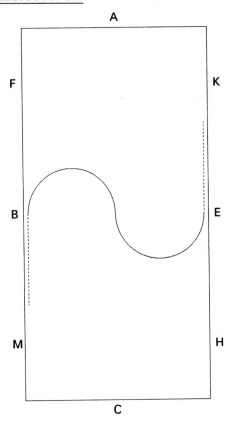

Explanation
Two half 10m circles commencing at either E or B, ridden in walk or sitting trot.

Likely problems
Track through X not straight.
Path does not go over X.
Semi-circles badly shaped.

Comment
Can be used as a change of rein.

EXERCISE 5.2

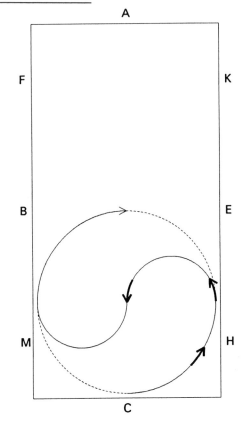

Explanation
Put the ride in closed order onto a 20m circle at one end of the school. Ride changes of rein within the circle by means of two half circles of 10m diameter. Can be ridden in walk or sitting trot.

Likely problems
Poor half circle shapes.

Comment
Useful way of changing the rein.

EXERCISE 5.3

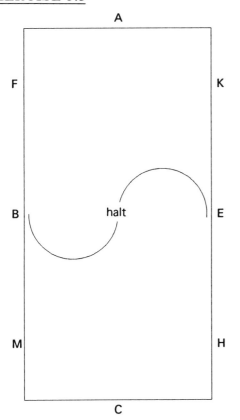

EXERCISE 5.4

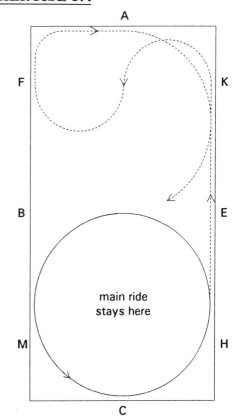

Explanation

Two half 10m circles, with a change of pace. Commence at B in walk and halt at X, then continue on the other rein to E. Have the rest of the ride halted on the M-H or F-K line.

Likely problems

Halt not square.

Halt not straight (i.e. not pointing directly at A or C).

Horse fidgets.

Second half circle poor shape.

Variation

Trot from B, walk before X, halt at X, then ride a transition from halt to trot on leaving X.

Explanation

Similar to Exercise 5.1, except that lead files individually go large, and perform the exercise away from the rest of the ride.

Lead file leaves the circle near H, performs two half circles of 10m diameter, and then takes rear file.

Likely problems

Same as those in Exercise 5.1.

New lead file tries to follow the horse doing the exercise.

EXERCISE 5.5

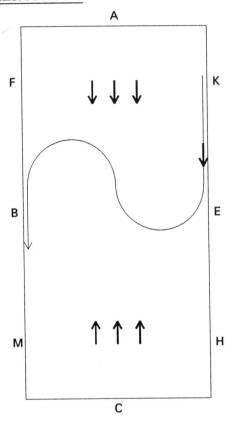

EXERCISE 5.6

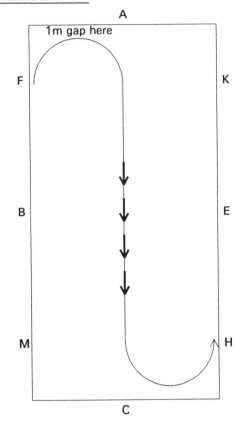

Explanation

Halt the ride on the F-K line. The line at M-H can also be used for larger classes. Each rider leaves the line-up in walk or trot, and commences two half 10m circles when he/she feels that the horse is listening to him/her.

Likely problems

Rider doesn't know when to commence the exercise.
Loss of rhythm.
Poor circle shapes.

Variation

Include canters between M and H, and between K and F.

Comments

Encourages independent riders.
Encourages a feeling for the horse.

Explanation

In walk or trot, ride a half 10m circle from F, go straight down the centre line to G, and ride a half 10m circle to H.

Likely problems

Ride meets the outer track at one short side.
Path down the centre line not straight.

Variation

Make the second half circle go from X to E.

Comment

This is quite a different exercise from 1.1 (a turn up the centre line from A).

EXERCISE 5.7

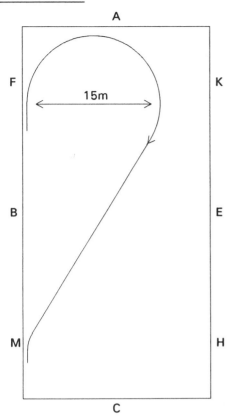

EXERCISE 5.8

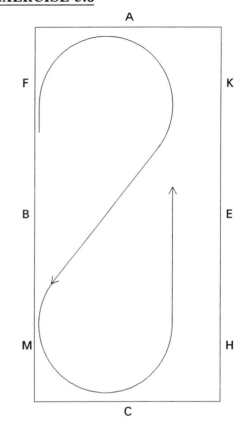

Explanation

Have the ride in closed order, going large in walk or trot on the outer track. Ride a 15m extended half circle, starting 2m before F.

Likely problems

Turn too soon late.
Poor circle shape.

Variations

Can be ridden in canter, introducing a small amount of counter-canter in the corner at M.
Can be ridden in reverse by more experienced rides.

Comment

The half circle should touch the threequarter line for exactly one stride.

Explanation

This is an extension of Exercise 5.7, including an additional 15m extended half circle after the incline. Should only be done in walk or trot. Note that the incline meets the long side of the school about 2m before M.

Likely problems

Horse not straight.
Poor shaped half circle at M.

Variation

Can be ridden in reverse.

EXERCISE 5.9

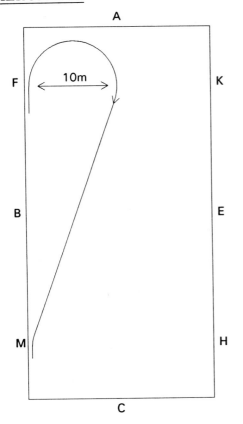

EXERCISE 5.10

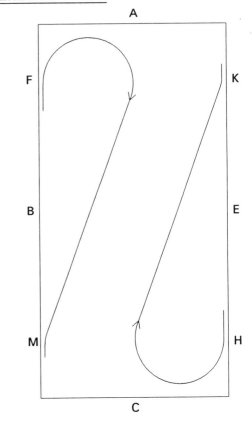

EXERCISE 5.9

Explanation
Similar to Exercise 5.7, except that an extended 10m half circle is used. If ridden in trot, the half circle must be ridden sitting.

Likely problems
Turn too soon/late.
Poor circle shape.

Variation
As with Exercise 5.7, can also be ridden in reverse.

EXERCISE 5.10

Explanation
Similar to Exercise 5.9. Divide the class into two rides, both on the same rein. Both rides perform a half circle and incline to change the rein.

Likely problems
One ride getting too close to the other along the incline.
One ride commences the exercise too early/late.

Variation
As with Exercises 5.7 and 5.9, can also be ridden in reverse.

EXERCISE 5.11

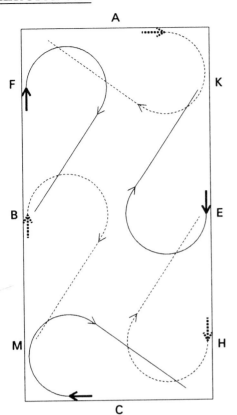

EXERCISE 5.12

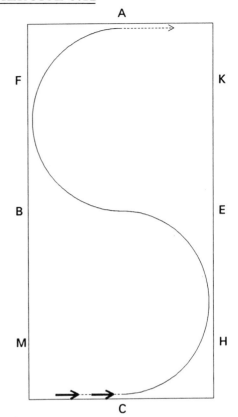

Explanation

Ride in open order as shown on the diagram in walk. Whole ride performs a simultaneous 10m half circle and incline back to the track. The riders at B and E must perform 9m half circles to avoid a collision.

Likely problems

Poor half circle shapes.
Some riders commence the exercise late.

Variations

Can be ridden in sitting trot.
Ride the exercise in reverse (i.e. ride the incline followed by the half circle).

Explanation

Have the ride walking or trotting in closed order, going large on the left rein. At C, lead file rides a half 20m circle left to X, followed by a half 20m circle right to A, with the rest of the ride following.

Likely problems

Ride may become lost the first time they attempt the figure.
Path misses X.
Path not straight over X.
Incorrect bend at the start of the second half circle.

Comment

This is a useful way of changing the rein with novice rides — once they have tried it a couple of times.

EXERCISE 5.13

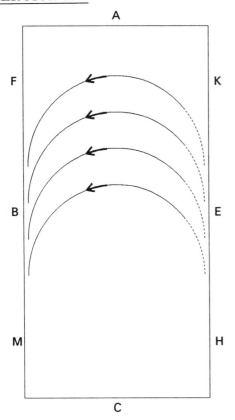

EXERCISE 5.14

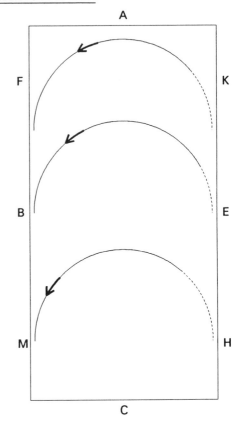

Explanation

Have the ride trotting in closed order, going large. On command, the whole ride simultaneously executes a half 20m circle from a long side. (This has the effect of reversing the order of the ride.)

Likely problems

Ride may become lost.
Turns not simultaneous.
Dressings deteriorate.

Variation

Can be ridden in walk for novice rides.

Comment

Useful prelude for the next exercise (5.14)

Explanation

Have the ride trotting in open order. Individual riders at will canter a half 20m circle from the HEK long side to the MBF long side, and then return to trot.

Safety!

Must only be attempted with a competent ride.
Before commencing the canter, each rider must check that there is a space available on the MBF long side.
Riders who are already on the MBF long side must give way to those doing the exercise.
Must never be done from both long sides at the same time (collision risk).

Likely problems

Wrong canter lead.
Poor transitions.

EXERCISE 5.15

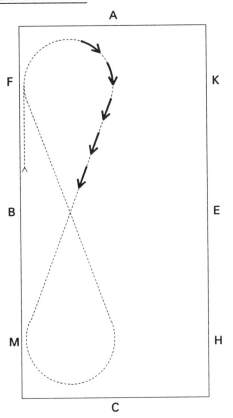

Explanation
Have the ride going large on the right rein in walk or sitting trot. On reaching F, commence a figure of eight in the MBF (long) half of the school. Execute two figures of eight and go large from F.

Likely problems
Ride becomes strung out.
Lines not straight.
Poor half circle shapes.
Riders cross the centre line.

Comment
Useful exercise if you have only a long half of the school in which to work.

6. *Serpentines*

Aims
Useful suppling exercise at the start of a lesson.
Encourages horses to soften to the rider's inside leg.
Encourages riders to obtain the correct bend in the horse.
Encourages riders to use their weight correctly.

General Points
The path of the serpentine divides the school into equal-sized loops.
Even numbers of loops always change the rein.
Odd numbers of loops never change the rein.
The half circle at the end of each loop is circular.
The path between each half circle is straight.
The width of each loop depends on the number of loops. For a 40m school:
    3 loops = 13.33m wide
    4 loops = 10m wide
    5 loops = 8m wide
    6 loops = 6.667m wide

Riding Serpentines
The rhythm and impulsion should remain
    the same throughout the exercise.
The horse should be bent through the half
    circles, and straight between the half
    circles.

How to Teach
Halt the ride (see diagram).
Walk the serpentine yourself.
Explain the aids as you go.
A shallow serpentine (see Exercise 6.1) is a
    useful introduction for novice riders.
Some blocks placed on the A-C line will help
    the riders (see diagram).

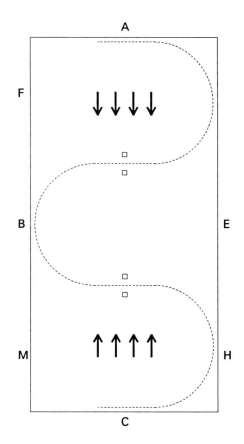

A SPECIMEN EXERCISE
The ride goes large, on the right rein, in sitting trot.
The ride commences a three-loop serpentine at A.

Preparations
Plan your track first.
Remind the riders of the aids if necessary.
Have your ride going large in sitting trot.
Stand away from the track and the path of the serpentine.
Give the words of command.

The Aids
Half-halt just before each half circle.
Inside rein shows the way.
Outside rein controls the impulsion.
Inside leg creates the impulsion.
Outside leg controls the horse's quarters.

The Command
'At A, the whole ride commence a three-loop serpentine, ride one serpentine, and then go large.'

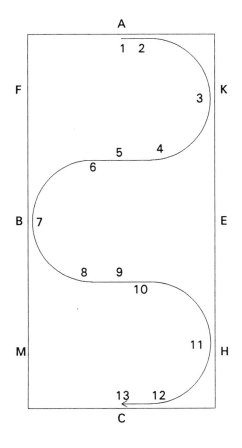

KEY
1. Good, active sitting trot.
2. Think of the shape of the half circle. Ask for position right.
3. Maintain a good shape to the circle.
4. Half-halt.
5. Ride straight.
6. Half-halt, position left.
7. Maintain a good shape to the circle.
8. Half-halt.
9. Ride straight.
10. Half-halt, position right.
11. Maintain a good shape to the circle.
12. Half-halt.
13. Ride straight.

EXERCISE 6.1

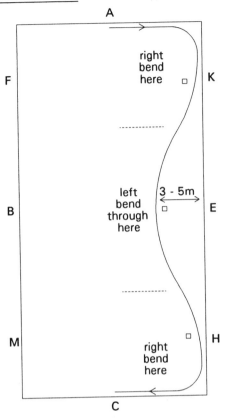

EXERCISE 6.2

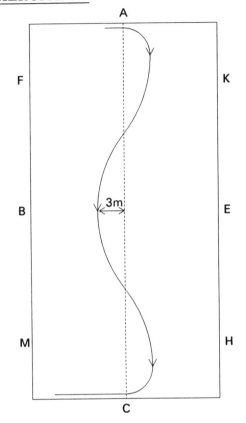

Explanation
Shallow loops off the long side in walk or trot. This is a suppling exercise for the horse and teaches the rider about changing the bend.

Likely problems
Rider not changing the bend correctly.
Rider's weight slipping out.
Loops too small (often) or too large (sometimes).

Comments
Can be used as a preparation for counter-canter.
Blocks can be used to help guide children and novice adults.

Explanation
Ride shallow loops along the centre line, with each of the loops about 3m away from line. Can be ridden in either closed or open order, and in walk or trot.

Likely problems
Late turns.
Uneven loops (either too wide or too long).

Variation
Riders can sometimes go large (this stops the horses anticipating).

EXERCISE 6.3

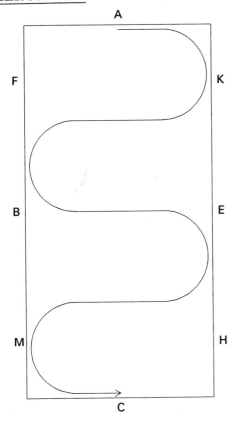

EXERCISE 6.4

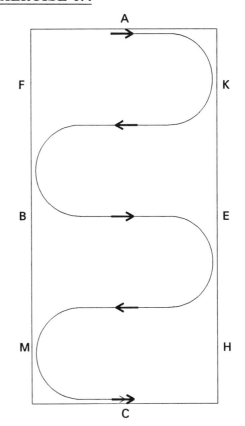

Explanation

The diagram shows a four-loop serpentine. The ride must (mentally) divide the school into four equal parts, of 10m each. Can be ridden in walk or trot.

Likely problems

Uneven sized loops.

Horse not straight when crossing the centre line.

Riders forget to change diagonal when in rising trot.

Variation

On completion of the first serpentine (from A), immediately commence another serpentine from C.

Explanation

This is similar to Exercise 6.3, but with some transitions included on the centre line. The transitions may be direct or progressive.

Lead file commences a four-loop serpentine at A, rear files halt at points on the centre line. When the whole ride has halted, rear files walk/trot and continue the serpentine. Each rider walks/trots as the ride reaches them, the whole ride going large at C.

Likely problems

Halting off the centre line.

Halting at an angle.

Riders moving off too soon/too late.

EXERCISE 6.5

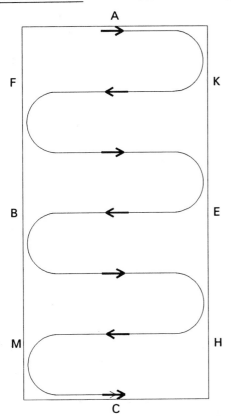

EXERCISE 6.6

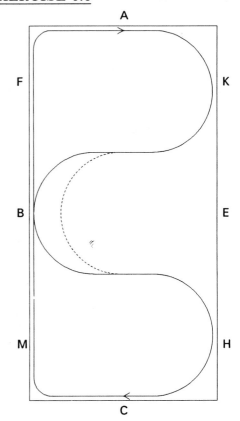

Explanation
A variation of Exercise 6.4, for a ride of up to seven with a six-loop serpentine. The size of the loops are too small for trot, and so must be ridden in walk — the loops are only 6.67m wide.

Explanation
Ride continuous three-loop serpentines from A, returning to A down a long side. Can be ridden in trot in either closed or open order. If in open order, the middle loop must be shallower.

Likely problems
Horses not bending correctly through the loops.
Horses not straight along the long side.

Variations
Can ask for some lengthened strides along the long side.
Canter along the MBF side.

EXERCISE 6.7

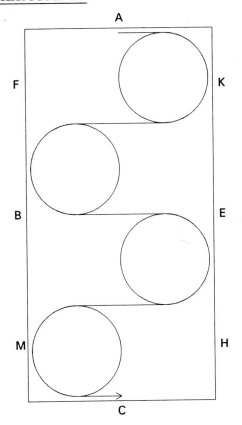

EXERCISE 6.8

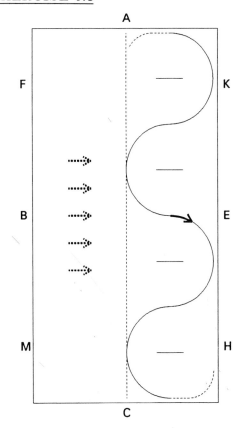

Explanation
Ride a four-loop serpentine in walk or trot, including a 10m circle in each of the loops. Suitable for rides of four riders maximum.

Likely problems
Ride becomes lost at the first attempt.
Poor circle shapes.
Incorrect bend in the horse, particularly at the start of each circle.
Loss of rhythm.

Explanation
Ride a four-loop serpentine in walk or trot in half the width of the school. Can be done individually, or as a ride. If trotted, must be sitting.

Likely problems
Incorrect bend for the first part of each half circle.
Poor shapes.
Loops uneven width.
Loops cross the centre line.

Comments
Can be used if you only have half a school in which to work.
Trotting poles between the loops (see diagram) will help the ride.

7. Leg Yielding

Aims
Useful preparation before embarking on other lateral work.
Encourages the horse to move away from the rider's leg.
Helps the rider's balance.

General Points
The leg yield is a movement away from the rider's leg.
The leg yield is **not** an incline.
When leg yielding in a straight line, a line drawn from the horse's hind feet to the fore feet is always parallel to a side of the school.
When leg yielding on a circle, the distance from the horse's fore feet to the centre of the circle is always matched by distance from the centre of the circle to the hind feet.
Leg yielding away from a long side is more difficult than leg yielding towards a long side.

Riding a Leg Yield
Care must be taken to avoid the horse being overbent.
The quarters must be guarded by the rider's inside leg to prevent them from 'trailing'.

How to Teach
Halt the ride.
Walk the track yourself.
Explain the aids.
For novice riders the first few attempts should be made with the riders starting no more than 2m away from the long side.

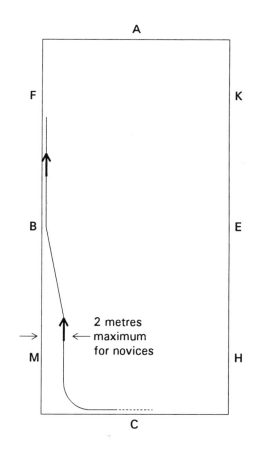

A SPECIMEN EXERCISE
The ride goes large, on the right rein, in trot, in open order.
On reaching C each rider goes forward to sitting trot.
Each rider turns onto the threequarter line after C.
After 10m, each rider commences a leg yield to the outer track.

Preparations
Plan your track first.
Remind the riders of the aids if necessary.
Have your ride going large in trot.
Stand away from the track and the threequarter line.
Give the words of command.

The Aids
Right rein asks for the bend.
Left rein opens and goes forward, establishing the direction of movement, and allowing the
  horse to bend, but still supporting the horse.
Right leg is applied on or behind the girth, asking for impulsion and moving the horse's
  hindquarters over.
Left leg is applied on the girth.
Weight is central or inside hip slightly forward.

The Command
'Each rider turn onto the threequarter line after C. Go straight for 10m, and commence a leg
yield to the left to the outer track.'

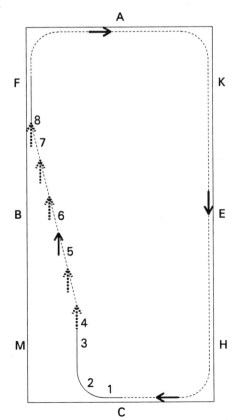

KEY
1. Good, active trot (sitting).
2. Good turn.
3. Half-halt.
4. Ask for the leg yield.
5. Keep the horse parallel to the boards.
6. Keep the rhythm.
7. Half-halt.
8. Forward, straight and large.

EXERCISE 7.1

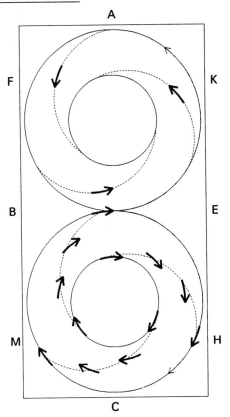

EXERCISE 7.2

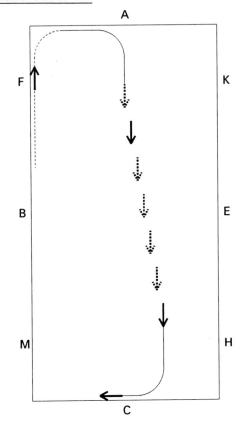

Explanation
Use the 20m circle for leg yielding exercises. Have the ride in trot in open order on a 20m circle, then spiral in to a 10m circle. On command, leg yield to the large circle.

Likely problems
Quality of the leg yield may be weak.
Poor circle shapes.

Comments
Staying too long on the small circle tires both riders and horses.

For large rides split into two rides, one at A, the other at C on the opposite rein, each rider passing through X.

The diagram shows spiralling in on the circle at A, and leg yielding out on the circle at C.

Explanation
Have the ride trotting in open order, going large on the right rein. At A, track right up the centre line. At D, leg yield left between 3m and 4m. On passing G, go straight. On reaching the end of the school, track left.

Likely problems
Poor turn.
Horse bent too far to the right.
Horse's hind legs don't cross.

EXERCISE 7.3

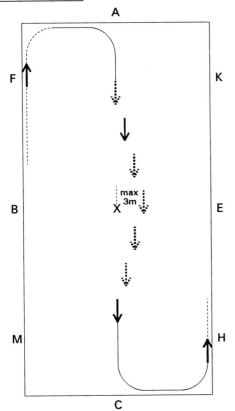

EXERCISE 7.4

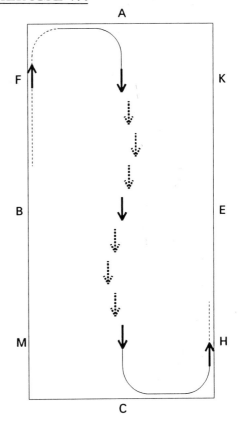

Explanation
Have the ride trotting in open order, going large on the right rein. At A, track right up the centre line. At D, leg yield left between 2m and 3m, going up as far as the B-E line, then leg yield right. On reaching C, change the rein.

Likely problems
Poor turn.
Horse bent too far left or right.
Horse's hind legs don't cross.
Leg yield too far from the centre line.
Late return to the centre line.

Explanation
This is a variation of the previous exercise (7.3), where each rider executes two smaller loops of leg yielding in trot, one on each side of X.

Likely problems
Loops different length (i.e. track does **not** cross X).
Loops different depth (i.e. distance from the centre line).

EXERCISE 7.5

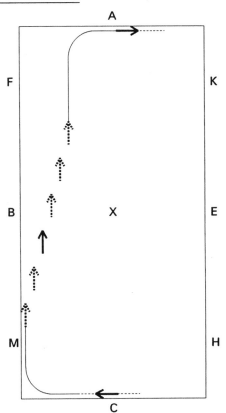

EXERCISE 7.6

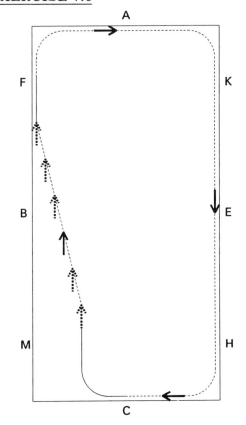

Explanation
Have the ride going large on the right rein in open order in trot. Just past M, each rider leg yields right to the threequarter line.

Likely problems
Horse hangs to the boards.
Horse turns onto the line instead of staying parallel to the boards.

Variation
Can leg yield away from the track on both long sides.

Comment
Leg yielding away from the side of the school is a much more demanding exercise than leg yielding towards the side of the school.

Explanation
This is a variation of the specimen exercise. Have the ride trotting in closed order on the right rein. As the front of the ride reaches the corner at F, lead file only goes forward to canter, and canters to the rear of the ride.

Safety!
The new lead file stays in trot on going past F until the first lead file has finished cantering.
Only to be attempted on rides where everybody is competent.

Variation
With the ride in open order, riders can canter F-A-K-E.

8. *Turn on the Forehand*

Aims

Progresses the rider's lateral balance.

Allows the rider to develop a better balance between leg and hand (otherwise the horse moves forwards or backwards, or the turn is not 'on the forehand'.)

Demonstrates greater collection produced by the rider.

General Points

The horse's fore feet stay within a 0.5m circle.

The horse's fore feet step up and down, marking time.

The horse's hind feet cross over during the exercise.

The horse is bent in the direction of the movement.

Riding a Turn on the Forehand

The initial halt should be square and 'active'.

The rhythm should remain the same throughout the exercise.

The horse should not become overbent.

The horse should move forward immediately the movement is complete.

How to Teach

Halt the ride.

Explain the aids.

Walk the track taken by the horse's hind legs, with yourself facing in same direction as the horse, so that your own legs cross.

Best started as a quarter turn, through 90 degrees (see Exercise 8.1).

The turn on the forehand should be taught to more advanced riders.

A SPECIMEN EXERCISE

The ride goes large, on the right rein, in trot, in open order.

On reaching E, the nominated rider tracks right towards B, and halts at X.

The nominated rider performs half a turn on the forehand to the right through 180 degrees, goes forward to trot, and goes large on the right rein.

The rest of the ride gives way at E if necessary.

Preparations

Remind the riders of the aids if necessary.

Have your ride going large in trot.

Stand away from the track and the line between E and X.

Give the words of command.

The Aids

Establish a square halt.

Right rein establishes the head and neck bend in the horse.

Left rein controls the impulsion.

Right leg stays on or behind the girth.

Left leg controls the quarters.

Weight remains central.

The Command

'On reaching E, [rider's name] track right to X, halt, ride a turn on the forehand to the right, go forward to trot, and on returning to E, track right.'

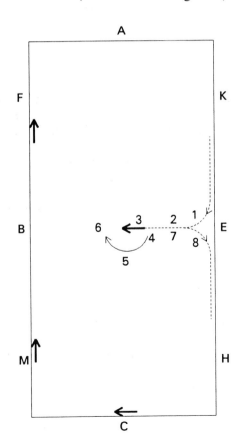

KEY
1. Good turn.
2. Straight.
3. Halt.
4. Ask for the turn.
5. Keep a good rhythm.
6. Immediately into trot.
7. Straight.
8. Good turn.

EXERCISE 8.1

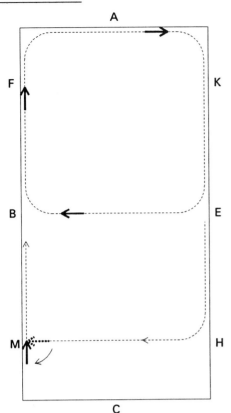

EXERCISE 8.2

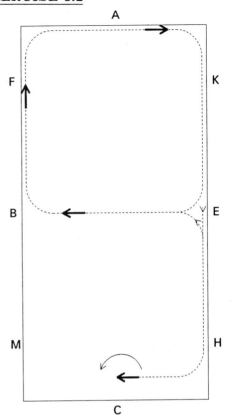

Explanation

Have the ride on the right rein on the 20m square at A. On command:

    individuals go large (from E);
    track right at H;
    halt facing M;
    execute a quarter turn on the forehand to the right;
    rejoin the ride.

Likely problems

Halt too close to the short side of the school.
Horse resists aids (put your hand on the quarters to assist!)
Too much head and neck bend in the horse.

Comment

The 90 degree turn is a useful introduction for novice riders.

Explanation

This exercise can be used when the riders have become proficient at the previous exercise (8.1). The ride is again going on the square at A. On command:

    individuals go large (from E);
    go onto the inner track after H;
    halt at C;
    ride a half turn on the forehand to the left;
    go large in trot;
    rejoin the ride.

Likely problems

Turn goes the wrong way (i.e. to the right).
Horse's hind legs don't cross.
Horse moves forward or backwards.
Loss of rhythm.
Loss of form, i.e. deterioration of the horse's outline.

EXERCISE 8.3

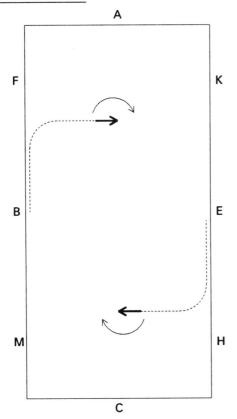

EXERCISE 8.4

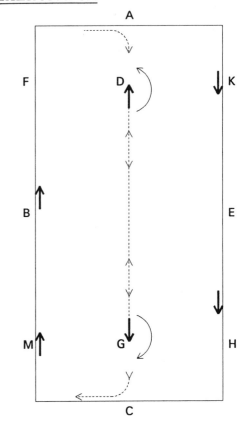

Explanation

Have the ride in open order, going large in trot. On command, riders turn from a long side, halt on the centre line, turn on the forehand in a named direction, trot, and go large.

Likely problems

Halt not square.
Halt not straight.
Horse walks a small circle.
Horse goes backwards.

Variation

Riders turn at will from either long side, and execute a turn on the forehand — should only be attempted with an advanced ride.

Explanation

Have the ride in open order, going large in trot on the right rein. On command, riders:
>   turn from A;
>   trot to G and halt;
>   execute half a turn on the forehand to the
>   right;
>   trot to D and halt;
>   execute half a turn on the forehand to the left;
>   trot to C and go large.

Likely problems

Poor turns.
Halts not at G and D.

EXERCISE 8.5

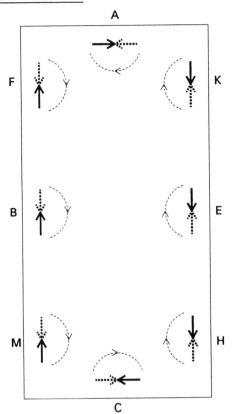

Explanation

Put the ride in walk going large in open order on the left rein. On command, the whole ride:

    goes onto the inner track;

    halts;

    does half a turn on the forehand;

    goes forward in trot.

Likely problems

Riders not coming far enough onto the inner track.

Riders turning the wrong way.

Some riders may finish before others. If so, those who have completed the exercise must avoid riders still performing it.

EXERCISE 8.6

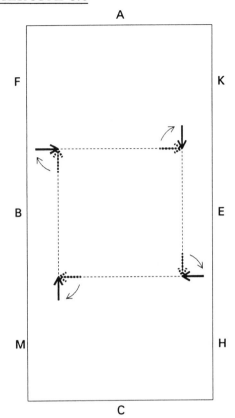

Explanation

This exercise can be used if there are no more than four riders in your class.

Put the ride in walk onto a 16m square in the middle of the school, and spread them out into open order. At every corner of the square, each rider does a quarter turn on the forehand.

Likely problems

Riders get too close to one another.

Square becomes mis-shaped.

Riders hurry the turns.

Comments

The square of 16m allows a 2m gap between two sides of the square and the long sides of the school. This gives the horses' hindquarters room during the turn.

This is a tiring exercise — keep it short.

EXERCISE 8.7

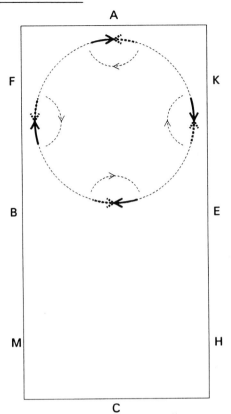

EXERCISE 8.8

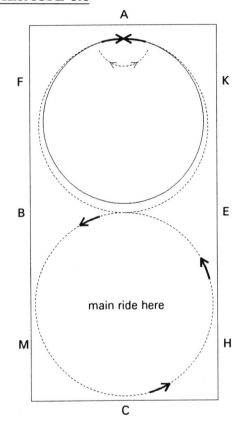

Explanation

Have the ride working in walk or trot on a 20m circle on the left rein in open order. On command, the whole ride comes onto an 18m circle, halts, and executes half a turn on the forehand.

Likely problems

Poor shape to the 18m circle.

Some riders finish the turn long after everybody else.

Riders turning the wrong way.

Comment

This is a useful way of changing the rein when working on 20m circle exercises.

Explanation

Have the ride walking or trotting a 20m circle at C in open order on the left rein. On command, a nominated rider:

   takes the right rein A circle;

   comes onto the inner track at A;

   halts, rides half a turn on the forehand;

   trots a circle back to A;

   halts, rides another half turn on the forehand;

   returns to the main ride.

Safety!

The person doing the exercise rides a slightly smaller A circle to avoid the rest of the ride at X.

Comment

To prevent boredom, the rest of the ride can be working on improving (for example):

   shape of the circle;

   depth of seat;

   rhythm;

   impulsion.

9. *Demi-pirouettes in walk*

Aims

Progresses the rider towards greater balance.
Improves the rider's weight-aid technique.
Improves tactful co-ordination of the aids.

General Points

The horse's hind feet stay within a 0.5m circle.
The horse's hind feet step up and down, marking time.
The horse's fore feet cross over during the exercise.
The horse is bent in the direction of the movement.

Riding a Demi-pirouette

The walk into the demi-pirouette should be impulsive and balanced.
The rhythm should remain the same throughout the exercise.
The horse should not become overbent.
The horse should move forward immediately the movement is complete.

How to Teach

Halt the ride.
Explain the aids.
As with the turn on the forehand, demonstrate the crossing of the forelegs yourself.
The demi-pirouette can be introduced as a series of progressively smaller arcs (see diagram).
The demi-pirouette is a more difficult exercise than a turn on the forehand.
Teach the demi-pirouette by asking for a turn through 90 degrees before progressing to 180 degrees.

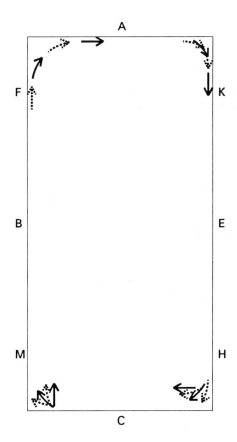

A SPECIMEN EXERCISE

The ride goes large, on the right rein, in trot, in open order.

On reaching A, the nominated rider tracks right towards X, and halts after D.

The nominated rider performs a demi-pirouette to the right, goes forward to trot, and goes large on the right rein.

The rest of the ride gives way at A if necessary.

Preparations

Remind the riders of the aids if necessary.

Have your ride going large in trot.

Stand away from the track and the line between A and X.

Give the words of command.

The Aids

Right rein establishes the head and neck bend in the horse.

Left rein controls the impulsion.

Right leg goes on the girth.

Left leg controls the quarters.

The Command

'On reaching A, [rider's name] track right to just past D, walk, ride a demi-pirouette to the right, go forward to trot, and on returning to A, track right.'

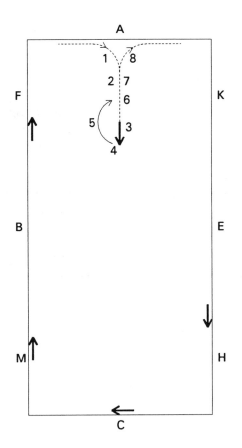

KEY

1. Good turn.
2. Straight.
3. Halt.
4. Ask for the demi-pirouette.
5. Keep a good rhythm.
6. Immediately into trot.
7. Straight.
8. Good turn.

EXERCISE 9.1

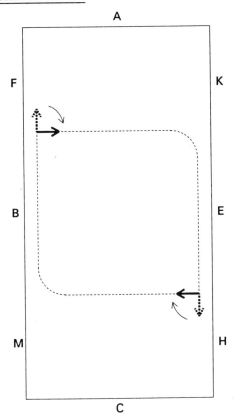

EXERCISE 9.2

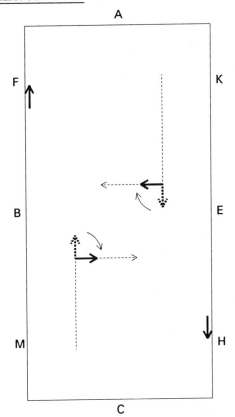

Explanation

Have the ride in open order, walking an 18m square about X. At the corners shown, individuals ride a quarter pirouette.

Likely problems

Riders become bunched (i.e. get too close to one another).

Horse's front legs don't cross.

Horse moves forwards or backwards.

Loss of rhythm.

Loss of form, i.e. outline.

Variation

If you have more than four riders, you can use two squares, one at A and another at C.

Explanation

Have the ride trotting large in open order. Riders turn onto either threequarter line at will, go forward to walk, ride a quarter pirouette, go forward to trot, rejoining the outer track.

Safety!

Riders must ensure that their quarter pirouette is clear of others who are doing the exercise.

Variation

You can have the ride walking large instead of trotting large — this is kinder to the less fit riders.

EXERCISE 9.3

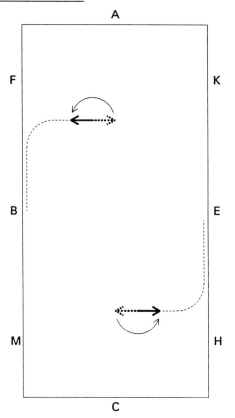

EXERCISE 9.4

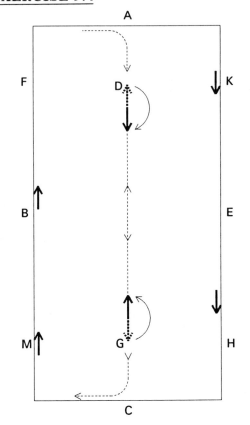

Explanation

Have the ride in open order, going large in trot. On command, riders turn from a long side, walk on the centre line, ride a demi-pirouette in a named direction, trot, and go large. This is similar to Exercise 8.3, except that it involves a demi-pirouette rather than a turn on the forehand.

Likely problems

Halt not square.
Halt not straight.
Horse walks a small circle.
Horse goes backwards.

Variation

Riders turn at will from either long side, and ride a demi-pirouette — should only be attempted with an advanced ride.

Explanation

Have the ride in open order, going large in trot on the right rein. On command, riders:
    turn from A;
    trot to G;
    ride a demi-pirouette to the right;
    trot to D;
    ride a demi-pirouette to the left in walk;
    trot to C;
    canter to the rear of the ride.
This is similar to Exercise 8.4, except that it involves a demi-pirouette rather than a turn on the forehand.

Likely problems

Poor turns.
Halts not at G and D.

10. *Rein-back*

Aims

Increases the horse's athletic ability.

Requires a greater degree of collection from the horse.

Useful when negotiating gates etc.

Useful if the horse has been accidentally 'boxed in' by others.

General Points

It is executed from the halt.

The halt should be square.

The halt should be 'active' (i.e. with the horse attentive to the rider).

At the end of the rein-back, the horse should move forward to either walk or trot.

The rein-back should be in a straight line.

The horse's feet work almost as diagonal pairs.

Riding a Rein-back

Ensure that the rider's weight is central.

The rider's legs are used as if asking for a walk.

The rider's hands indicate a movement towards the rear.

The rider's hands must not 'drag the horse backwards'.

How to Teach

Explain the aids.

Explain the points of the rein-back.

Assist the horse by placing a hand on his chest if either the horse is green, or the rider is giving unclear aids.

See Exercise 10.1 for a useful first lesson in the rein-back.

A SPECIMEN EXERCISE

The ride is halted in open order on the outer track.
On command, every rider rides two steps of rein-back, and then goes forward immediately
    into trot.

Preparations

Spread the ride into open order.
Halt individual riders at nominated markers.
Remind the riders of the aids if necessary.
Stand somewhere where you can see everybody, usually in a corner, but outside the school is
    safer.
Give the words of command.

The Aids

Both legs on the girth ask for a walk.
Both hands squeeze the reins to indicate 'rearwards'.
The rider's seat lightens.

The Command

'Whole ride prepare to ride a rein-back. [Pause.] Whole ride commence.'

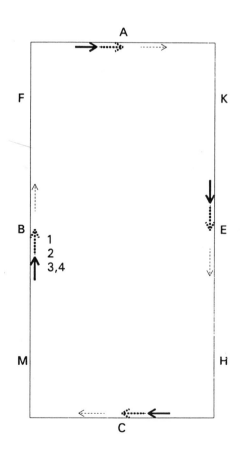

KEY
1. Square, 'active' halt.
2. Straight back.
3. Good transition.
4. Active trot.

EXERCISE 10.1

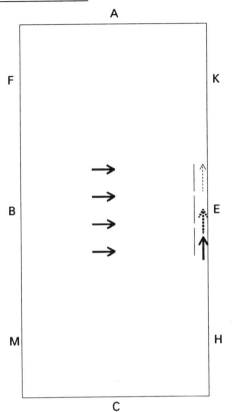

EXERCISE 10.2

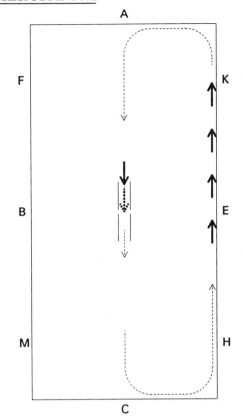

Explanation

Place two or three poles parallel to the side of the school. Halt the ride near the AXC line. Riders individually walk from H to E, halt at E, ride two steps of rein-back, go forward to trot, and rejoin the ride.

Likely problems

Rein-back not straight.
Loss of rhythm.
Horse doesn't move back.

Comment

A hand on the horse's shoulder or chest often helps novices.

Explanation

Place four poles around the X marker (see diagram). Halt the ride on a long side. Riders individually walk to X, halt, rein-back, and then trot to the rear of the ride.

Likely problems

Rein-back not straight.
Loss of rhythm.

Variation

The rest of the ride could be in walk or trot.

EXERCISE 10.3

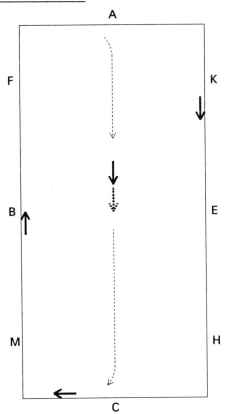

Explanation
Have the ride in open order in walk or trot. A named rider turns onto the centre line from A or C, halts at X for two seconds, reins back three steps, goes forward to trot, and returns to the outer track.

Likely problem
Riders already on the track must give way to the person completing the exercise.

Comment
This is more advanced than any of the previous rein-back exercises.

11. *Trotting Poles*

Aims
Essential preparation before teaching a novice horse or rider to jump.
Increases the horse's athletic ability.
Helps to settle a horse's rhythm into a fence.
Can be used to help place both horse and rider before a fence.

General Points
There should always be at least three poles (for safety).
The distance between the poles is usually 1.2m (4ft) to 1.5m (5ft), depending upon the size of the pony or horse. Further adjustment may be necessary when working with very large horses or very small ponies — see distance chart in Chapter 12.

Riding Trotting Poles
The turn before the trotting poles is just as important as the rest of the exercise.
The rhythm and impulsion should remain the same throughout the exercise.
The horse may attempt to return immediately to the others after negotiating the last pole.

How to Teach
Halt the ride (see diagram).
Check girths.
Check stirrups.
Explain the importance of the shortened stirrups.
Walk the track, explaining the aids and rider's position as you go.
For novice lessons, have the rest of the ride in halt while one person does the exercise (for safety).
Check and replace trotting poles which have been kicked.

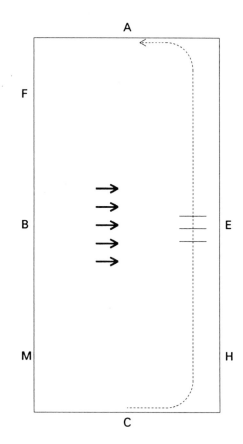

A SPECIMEN EXERCISE

The ride goes large, on the left rein, in open order.

Upon command, one rider turns after the C marker, and goes over three trotting poles. The rest of the ride follows.

Preparations

Put the trotting poles near E, but at least 2m (6ft 6ins) clear of the side of the school to allow following riders to avoid them in case they are kicked out of place.

Check the distances between the poles.

Check that the poles are parallel.

Check that the riders have shortened their stirrups.

Remind the riders of the aids if necessary.

Stand away from the track and the approach and get-away paths.

Give the words of command.

The Command

'After C, [rider's name] track left, go over the trotting poles, ride straight to the end of the school, and continue large; the rest of the ride following.'

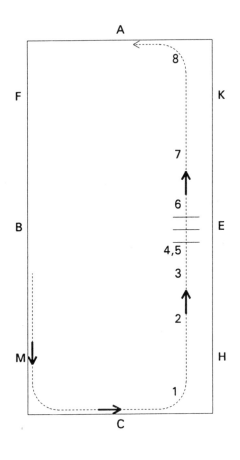

KEY
1. Good turn.
2. Ride straight.
3. Go into forward position.
4. Look up and ahead.
5. Allow with the reins.
6. Sit up.
7. Keep straight.
8. Good turn.

EXERCISE 11.1

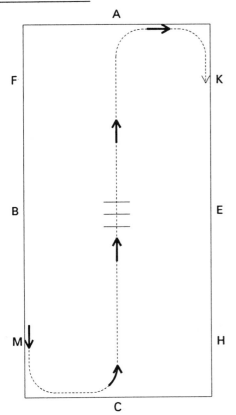

EXERCISE 11.2

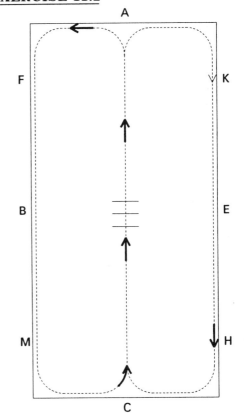

Explanation
Have the ride in open order, turning onto the centre line at C. Change the rein every time at A.

Likely problems
Poor turns (before and after).
Approach not straight.
Get-away not straight.
Rider looks down.
Track misses the centres of the poles.
Two foot falls between poles.
Horse stumbles.
Loss of rhythm and/or impulsion.
Riders turning onto the wrong rein at A.

Variation
Can be extended to five trotting poles.

Explanation
Similar to Exercise 11.1, except that each rider goes the opposite way to the person in front of him when he reaches A.

Likely problem
Riders turning the wrong way.

Comment
If you have an even number of riders, you must nominate someone as a 'lead file' to change the rein every time at A.

EXERCISE 11.3

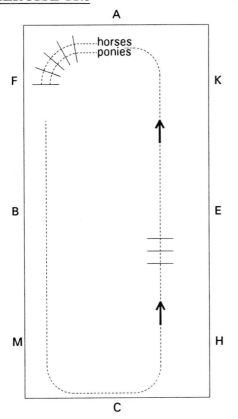

EXERCISE 11.4

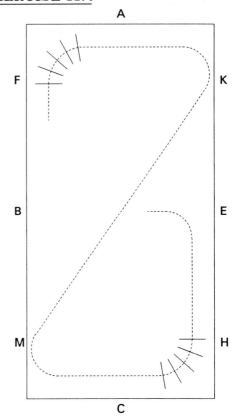

Explanation
Put some trotting poles along one side of the school, and some through a corner. Have the ride in open order, going over both sets of poles. In the corner, ponies should cross them more towards the X end of the poles, larger horses more towards the edge of the school.

Likely problem
Riders choosing a poor path through the trotting poles near F.

Comment
Helps the riders to feel how the horse goes when using different length strides.

Explanation
Use two sets of poles in diagonally opposite corners, working the ride in semi-open order through rein changes and transitions.

Likely problem
Riders getting too close to one another.

Variations
Include transitions.
Try some lengthening of stride across the diagonal.

Comments
Make sure that the distances at the centre of the poles is correct (1.4-1.5m/4ft 6ins-5ft).
Going wider encourages lengthening of stride.

EXERCISE 11.5

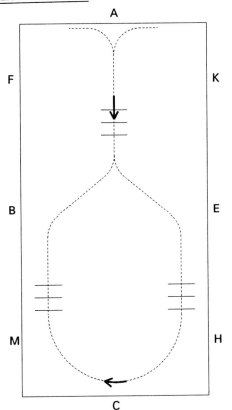

EXERCISE 11.6

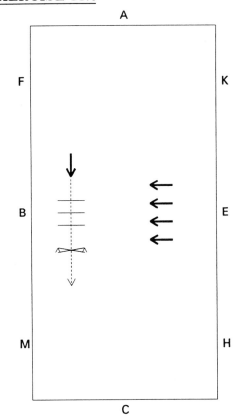

Explanation

Place a set of trotting poles on the centre line, and two sets off the outer track. Move the ride round the school in open order, sometimes using the poles. The track shown is only by way of example.

Likely problem

Poor turns into the poles.

Variations

Sometimes go large and work on transitions. Work on one or two sets of poles at a time.

Comment

The example drawn is good fun for ponies.

Explanation

Halt the ride on the threequarter line. Have individual riders come over the trotting poles, and the jump at the end.

Likely problem

Loss of impulsion.

Comments

This is useful if the ride needs a rest (children and older riders).

Can keep the ride in open order if everybody is fit.

Useful as an introduction to jumping.

12. *Jumps and Courses*

General Points
The fence should always be jumped in the middle.
Neither horse nor rider can influence the flight once the horse's hind feet have left the ground.

Riding a Jump
The turn before the jump is **just as important** as the rest of the exercise.

How to Teach

Always:
For novice riders, halt the ride. Check girths and stirrups yourself.
For more advanced riders, the ride may be left in walk. Have the riders check their own girths and stirrups.
Never have more than one person jumping at any time.

For single fences:
Remind everybody of the aids, and of the importance of the track.

For related fences and place poles:
Check the distances (see the next page for these).

For courses:
Walk the course yourself, checking the size of all turns, and the approach and get-away tracks.
Have the ride jump fences individually, then combine into a course.

Safety of Fences
Individual fences should always be designed for safety. The main points are:
  Dropper poles always go in front of the horizontal pole if the two poles share the same cup.
  Spread fences should always be approached so that its lowest part is jumped first (except hog's backs).
  If you have a 'gate', make sure that the gate supports are in the cups, and **never** in front of the wings.
  Ground lines should always be slightly in front of the plane of the first element of any jump, and **never** behind that plane.
And never leave unused jump cups in a jump wing.

Related Fence Distances

The distance between related fences must be set according to the height and ability of the horses in your class. This could be anything from 12hh to 17hh.

	12hh	15hh	17hh
Trotting poles	1.06m (3ft 6ins)	1.4m (4ft 6ins)	1.6m (5ft 6ins)
Trot pole to cross pole	1.8-2.4m (6-8ft)	2.4-3.05m (8-10ft)	3.05-3.6m (10-12ft)
Bounce			
trot approach	2.1-2.4m (7-8ft)	2.7-3.05m (9-10ft)	3.3-3.6m (11-12ft)
canter approach	2.4-2.7m (8-9ft)	3.05-3.3m (10-11ft)	3.6-3.9m (12-13ft)
Double, one non-jumping stride			
trot approach	4.2-4.8m (14-16ft)	5.2-5.7m (17-19ft)	6.1-6.7m (20-22ft)
canter approach	5.2-5.7m (17-19ft)	6.1-6.7m (20-22ft)	7-7.6m (23-25ft)
Double, two non-jumping strides			
trot approach	7-7.6m (23-25ft)	8.2-8.8m (27-29ft)	9.4-10m (31-33ft)
canter approach	7.9-8.5m (26-28ft)	9.1-9.7m (30-32ft)	10.3-10.9m (34-36ft)

All distances are calculated from the rearmost pole of one fence to the first pole (excluding any ground line) of the next fence.

While Building a Course

More advanced rides will want to keep moving while you are building the course. The diagrams below show some of the exercises that they could use. They would be carried out in walk for the less fit rides, or they could be trotted by the fitter rides.

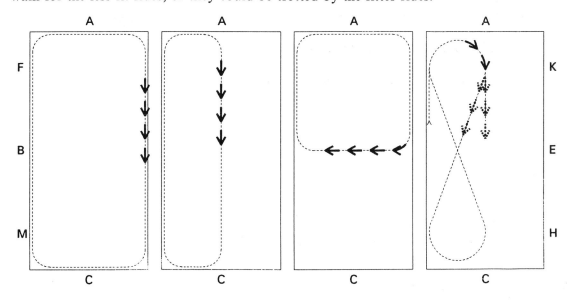

A SPECIMEN EXERCISE

All the riders are near the centre line, facing B.

A nominated rider goes forward to walk and trot on the left rein.

This rider trots large for at least one complete circuit of the school, then turns after A and jumps the bounce fence.

Preparations

Remind the riders of the aids if necessary.

Halt the ride near the centre line (see diagram).

Stand away from the track and the approach and get-away lines.

Give the words of command.

The Aids

Approaching the fence

Both reins have an even and steady contact.

Both legs applied equally on the girth to move the horse forward in a straight line.

Fold forward as the horse's front legs leave the ground.

Push the reins towards the bit.

Bouncing and landing

Sit up, so that you are upright when the hind feet hit the ground.

Regain the rein contact, and keep it even.

Apply legs evenly on the girth and keep horse straight, ready for second element.

Ride a straight get-away.

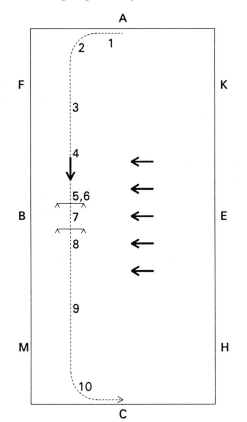

The Command

'[Rider's name] go forward to walk. On reaching the outer track, track left. On reaching M, go forward to trot. On reaching A, complete one circuit of the school. On returning to A, turn left, and jump the fence.'

KEY

1. Impulsive, but unhurried, trot.
2. Good turn.
3. Ride straight.
4. Keep the tempo.
5. Fold forward, and allow with the hands.
6. Look up!
7. Sit up and fold again.
8. Sit up.
9. Ride straight.
10. Ride a good turn.

EXERCISE 12.1

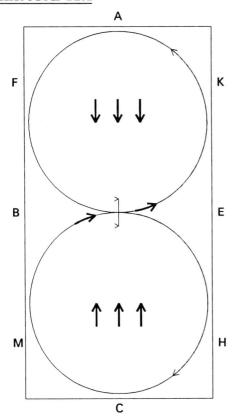

EXERCISE 12.2

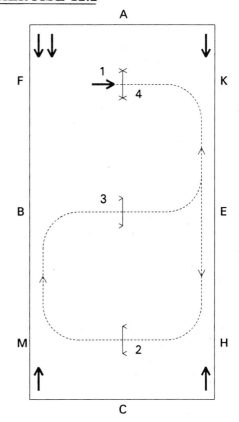

Explanation
Halt the ride as shown in the diagram. Each rider in turn rides a figure of eight over a jump at X. Can be ridden in trot or canter.

Likely problems
Approach not straight.
Wrong leading leg on landing.
Poor circle shapes.

Comment
Useful for teaching how to give a correct canter lead signal to the horse.

Explanation
Halt the riders in each of the corners. Have one rider at a time come out of his corner, and jump a three-loop serpentine. Can be ridden in either trot or canter.

Likely problems
Poor turns into the fences.
Rider not looking for the next fence.

Comment
This exercise is not suitable for large or stiff horses, nor for novice riders. See Exercise 12.3 for a course which is more suitable.

EXERCISE 12.3

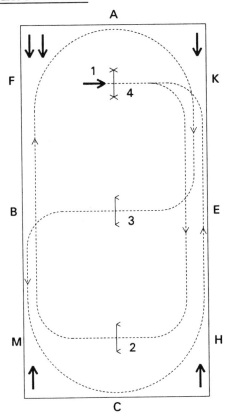

EXERCISE 12.4

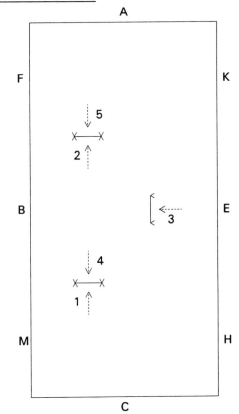

Explanation
An alternative course for the fences used in Exercise 12.2, and suitable for large or stiff horses and novice riders. Follow the sequence 1 to 4 shown in diagram.

Explanation
Another simple arrangement using only three jumps. Approaches can be in either trot or canter.

Likely problem
Run out to the right at fence 4.

Comment
If fences 1 and 2 are any closer, make sure that they are set at a related distance suitable for the size of horses/ponies in the ride.

EXERCISE 12.5

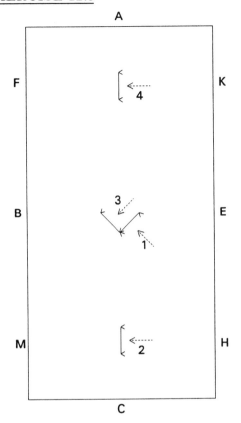

Explanation
This is a simple course using only four jumps. Best worked with trot approaches to each jump. The course shown can be worked in canter with more advanced rides.

Likely problems
Run out to the right at fences 1 and 3.
Poor turns into fences 2 and 4.

Variations
Jump the course backwards, or in a different order. See the diagrams below.

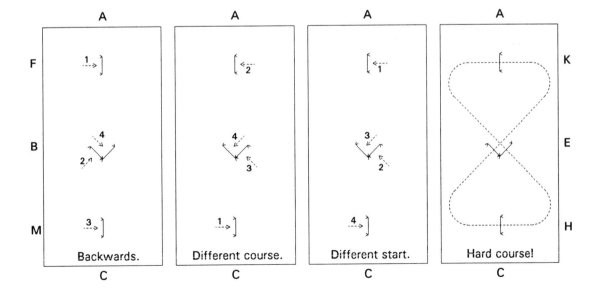

Backwards.   Different course.   Different start.   Hard course!

EXERCISE 12.6

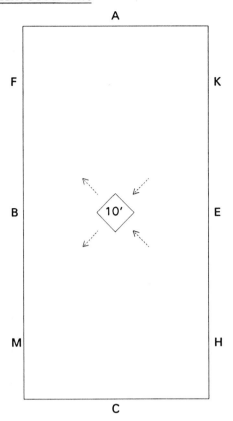

EXERCISE 12.7

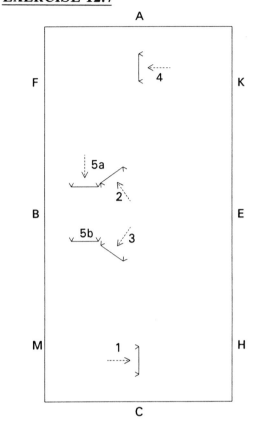

Explanation

Halt the ride in the corners of the school. Individual riders jump a figure of eight over the bounce centred on X. Approach in trot.

Likely problems

Lack of impulsion into the fences.
Corners (HFKM) not used.

Variations

Spread one pair of fences to make a 1 non-jumping stride double. Make distance suitable for trot or canter approach and specify pace to be ridden.
Make the first fence a cross pole.

Explanation

A simple course of fences incorporating a double. Approaches can be in trot or canter.

Likely problems

Wrong canter lead on landing.
Run out or stop at fence 5 (loss of impulsion through the turn after fence 4).

Variation

Fence 5 can be made a bounce.

EXERCISE 12.8

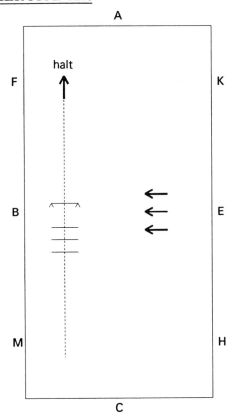

EXERCISE 12.9

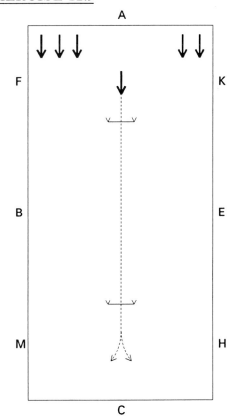

Explanation

Halt the ride on the threequarter line, facing B. Riders individually trot over the trotting poles, jump the fence, and halt near F.

Likely problem

Halt not executed.

Comment

Teaches riders to regain control as soon as possible after landing.

Explanation

Halt the ride in the corners near A. From a trot approach, riders individually jump the two fences shown, landing on a named lead after the second fence, and continuing large.

Likely problem

Wrong canter lead.

Comment

Useful for showing if a rider is using the weight aids correctly.

EXERCISE 12.10

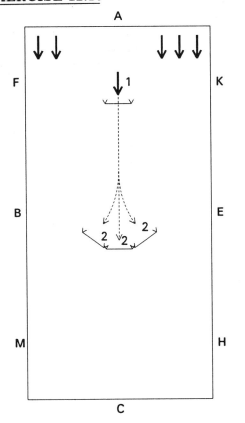

EXERCISE 12.11

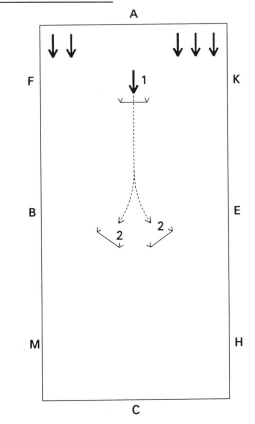

Explanation
Halt the ride in the corners near F and K. Riders individually jump the fence near D, and go over the fence nominated by the instructor. Approach the first fence in trot.

Likely problem
Jumping the wrong fence.

Explanation
Similar to Exercise 12.10, but with the centre fence removed.

Likely problem
Run out between the second fences.

EXERCISE 12.12

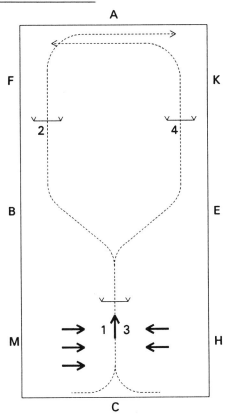

Explanation

Halt the ride as shown in the diagram. Riders individually jump the course shown, working out of trot into fences 1 and 3, and out of canter into fences 2 and 4.

Likely problems

Failure to establish canter.
Incorrect canter lead.
Run out at fences 2 and 4.

Comment

Useful for establishing that the rider is asking for the correct canter lead over a fence.

13. *Double Ride Work*

Aims

Encourages riders to be aware of where other riders are within the arena.

Improves the riders' control of speed, rhythm and impulsion.

Improves the riders' figure work.

Useful preparation for riders working independently within the arena.

Provides practice for demonstrations and displays at events such as Christmas shows.

General Points

The second lead file dresses to the first lead file.

The remainder of the odd-numbered ride dresses to the rider in front of them; the remainder of the even-numbered ride dress to the rider in front of them and to their partners in the other ride.

Working in Double Rides

Most double ride work is ridden in trot but exercises can be practised in walk first, then ridden in trot.

Whenever the rides meet, always pass left-hand to left-hand, except in special manoeuvres.

How to Teach

Ensure that every rider has sufficient control to be safe before attempting these exercises.

Practice all but the simplest movements in walk before attempting them in trot or canter.

It is more important to use clear and precise words of command in these exercises than in any other type of exercise.

A SPECIMEN EXERCISE
Have the class working as two rides, both rides going large, one ride on each rein, both rides
    trotting.
On reaching A, both rides turn towards C, and ride as a double ride up the centre line.
On reaching C, the rides divide, each going onto its original rein.

Preparations
Number off the ride.
On reaching A, the ride turns towards C.
On reaching C, the even numbers track right, the odd numbers track left.
Whenever the rides meet, they pass left-hand to left-hand.
Give the words of command.

The Command
'On reaching A, both rides track towards C, ride as a double ride to C, and on reaching C,
divide, returning to your original reins.'

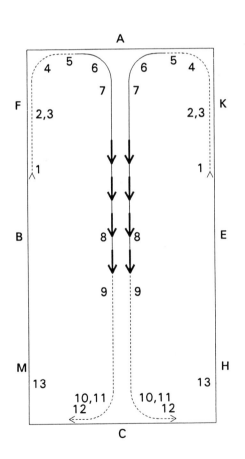

KEY
1. Ensure a steady tempo.
2. Lead files check dressings.
3. Everybody else check dressings.
4. Good turns.
5. Keep the tempo.
6. Good turns.
7. Check dressings.
8. Ride straight.
9. Check dressings.
10. All the way to C.
11. Good turns.
12. Keep the tempo.
13. Check dressings.

EXERCISE 13.1

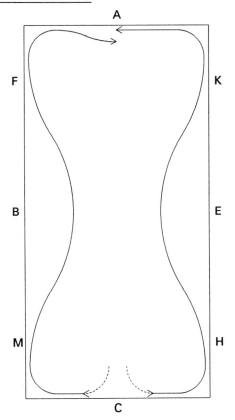

EXERCISE 13.2

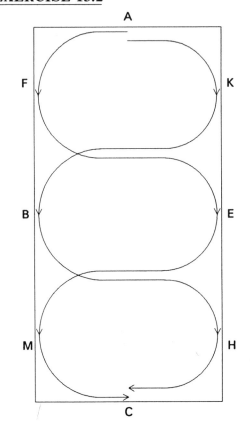

Explanation
Divide the ride by an appropriate means (the specimen exercise will do). Both rides walk or trot a shallow loop down the long sides.

Likely problems
Loops different widths.
Dressings go wrong near F and K.

Variation
Ride can go on to do another loop down the next long side.

Explanation
Two interlocking serpentines can be used for double ride work. It is important to keep both rides in closed order, with everybody passing left to left. Walk or trot exercise only.

Likely problems
Riders passing too close to one another.
Dressings may drift.
Rides can become lost unless you have two good lead files.

Comments
Best done with an even number of riders.
Six riders is the most you can usually get away with — if you want to do it with eight, they must **all** be very good.

EXERCISE 13.3

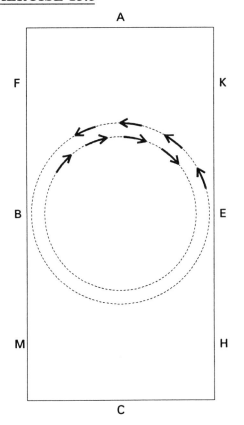

EXERCISE 13.4

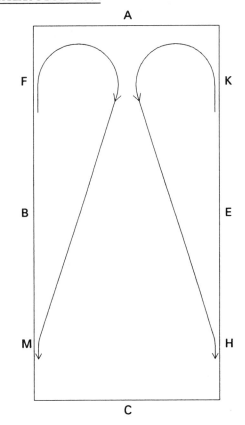

Explanation
With both rides in closed order on opposite reins, simultaneously commence two circles from B and E. The rides pass left-hand to left-hand as they cross the centre line. The riders on the inner circle must keep the same impulsion as the other ride, but they must ride with a slower speed. Can be ridden in either walk or trot.

Likely problems
Riders forget to pass left-to-left.
Poor circle shapes where the two rides pass at the centre line.
The inner ride goes round the circle faster.

Variation
Can be done in open order.

Explanation
With both rides on opposite reins, simultaneously ride a half circle and incline back to the track from F and K. Can be ridden in walk or trot but if trotted, the half circle must be ridden sitting.

Likely problems
Half circles unequal size.
Half circles not equidistant from the A-C line.
One or two horses may use the other ride as an excuse to be naughty.

EXERCISE 13.5

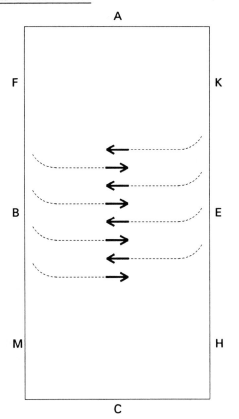

EXERCISE 13.6

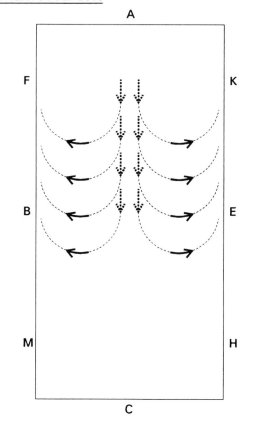

Explanation
Both rides turn simultaneously from both long sides, and ride through one another on the A-C line. Can be ridden in walk or trot.

Likely problems
Spacings between horses uneven as the rides cross.
Rides not straight on the A-C line.

Variation
Can include a transition on or before the A-C line.

Comments
If both rides change the rein, the order of riders is preserved, otherwise they are reversed.
If one ride changes the rein, then both rides will be on the same rein (useful for some exercises).

Explanation
Both rides come down the A-C line in either trot or walk, and simultaneously ride half 9m circles to the long sides of the school. This leaves both rides on their original reins.

Likely problem
Turns not simultaneous.

EXERCISE 13.7

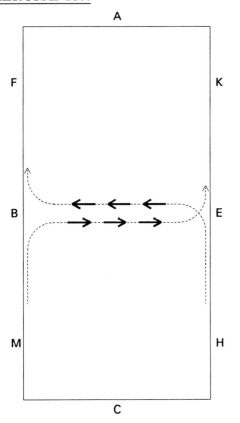

Explanation

This is a means of changing the rein. Can be ridden in trot or walk.

Likely problems

Tracks not equidistant from the B-E line.
Riders don't cross at X.

EXERCISE 13.8

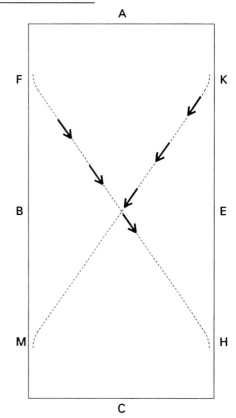

Explanation

Spread both rides out so that there is about one and a half to two horses' distance between riders (about 4m). Both rides change the rein across the long diagonals, passing through one another at X.

Safety!

Best limited to walk and trot.

Likely problems

Tracks don't cross at X.
Riders unevenly spaced.

EXERCISE 13.9

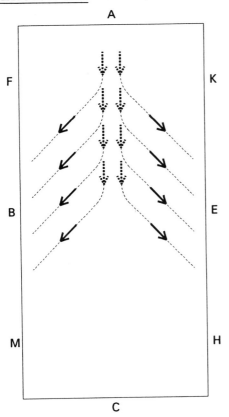

Explanation
Both rides come down the A-C line in either walk or trot, and simultaneously turn to the long sides of the school. This changes the rein for both rides.

Likely problems
Turns not simultaneous.
Angles ridden to the boards unequal.

Comment
When this exercise is done as part of an exhibition ride, everybody needs to turn on the signal of the lead file.

Cross-Reference to Exercises

The numbers given for each category refer to **Exercise numbers** (not page numbers).

CANTER
2.14   2.15   2.16
3.6   3.10   3.11
5.7   5.14
12.1

CIRCLES
Chapter 3
Chapter 4
5.2
6.7
7.1   8.8
12.1

EXHIBITION RIDING
2.5   2.18
5.10   5.13
8.5   8.7
Chapter 13

EXPERIENCED RIDERS
1.3
2.8   2.9   2.15 2.16 2.17 2.18
3.5   3.6   3.10 3.11
4.5   4.6   4.9
5.1   5.2   5.3   5.4   5.5   5.6   5.11 5.14
6.3   6.4   6.5   6.6   6.7
Chapters 7-10 inclusive
11.5
12.4 12.11
13.2

HALF A SCHOOL
3.1   3.12
4.1   4.2   4.8   4.10
5.2   5.15
6.9
8.7

LENGTHENING OF STRIDE
2.11

NOVICE RIDERS
1.1   1.2   1.4
2.1   2.3   2.4   2.7   2.17
3.1   3.7   3.8   3.9   3.12
4.2
5.6   5.12
11.1   11.3   11.6
12.8   12.9

OPEN ORDER
2.6   2.7   2.8   2.9   2.10   2.16
3.3
4.4   4.6
5.11
6.4   6.5
Chapters 7-9 inclusive
11.1   11.2   11.3

TRANSITIONS
2.8   2.10   2.11   2.16   2.17
3.3   3.7   3.11
4.8
5.3   5.14
Chapter 10
12.8

Bibliography

BRITISH HORSE SOCIETY: *The Instructor's Handbook*, 5th edition, 1985.
BRITISH HORSE SOCIETY: *The Manual of Horsemanship*, 9th edition, 1989.
BRITISH SHOW JUMPING ASSOCIATION: *Notes on Course Designing for Show Jumping Competitions.*
SIVEWRIGHT, MOLLY: *Thinking Riding, Book 1*, J.A. Allen, 1979.

PROGRESSIVE SCHOOL EXERCISES
for
DRESSAGE & JUMPING

A Handbook for
Instructors and Riders

ISLAY AUTY BA, FBHS

Progressive School Exercises provides a collection of exercises, on the flat and over fences, specifically designed for use in training **more experienced riders** and **horses**, whether in groups or as individuals, or schooling at home. Specially chosen ridden exercises aim to improve:

IN THE HORSE – rhythm, impulsion, balance, elasticity, straightness, athleticism, suppleness, obedience and self-carriage

IN THE RIDER – balance, effectiveness, accuracy, co-ordination, forward planning, 'feel', and the ability to 'see a stride' when jumping

The book is divided into groups of related exercises, each accompanied by a full description, the relevant aids, teaching hints, and advice on remedying typical faults.

Exercises include:
loops and circles • movements with transitions
work on diagonal lines • moving away from the leg
leg yield • developing canter
counter canter • shoulder-in
jumping exercises over grids, doubles and related distances